EDWARDS
Air Force Base
Experimental Flight Test Center

Steve Pace

Motorbooks International
Publishers & Wholesalers ®

Dedication

*In memory of all government and civilian flight-test pilots, flight-test engineers, flight-test
navigators, and flight-test crew members who paid the dearest price of all to propel America
to the forefront of aero-space achievement throughout the last half-century;
this work is dedicated to them and to their survivors.*

First published in 1994 by Motorbooks International
Publishers & Wholesalers, PO Box 2, 729 Prospect
Avenue, Osceola, WI 54020 USA

Library of Congress Cataloging-in-Publication Data
    Pace, Steve.
      Edwards AFB experimental flight test center/
    Steve Pace.
        p. cm.
      Includes bibliographical references and index.
      ISBN 0-87938-869-2
        1. Edwards Air Force Base (Calif.)—History.
    2. Airplanes—California—Edwards Air Force
Base—Flight testing—History.
    I. Title.
    TL568.E34P33   1994
    623.7'46'0973—dc20   94-1459

On the front cover: Paul Bikle (center), former director
of NASA's Dryden Flight Research Facility, and five of
the twelve X-15 pilots. The pilots are, from left to right,
USAF Maj. Joe Engle, NASA's Milt Thompson, USAF
majors Robert Rushworth and Pete Knight, and NASA
pilot John McKay. *NASA*

On the back cover: *Main photo:* Famed Lockheed test
pilot Tony LeVier poses atop the Lockheed XF-104.
Lockheed Lower left photo: The USAF's Ryan-built X-13
Vertijet hovers by it launch and recovery device.
Teledyne Ryan Aeronautical Lower right photo: The
number one B-1B in the AFFTC's Anechoic Chamber at
Edwards AFB. *Rockwell via Chris Wamsley*

Printed and bound in the United States of America

Contents

Acknowledgments

I greatly appreciate the contributions to this reference by the following: chief historian Dr. James O. Young and deputy historian Cheryl Gumm, Air Force Flight Test Center History Office; Don Nolan, NASA Ames-Dryden Flight Research Facility public affairs; Chris Wamsley; Tony Landis Photography; Mike Machat Illustration; Randy Cannon; Tom Rosquin; Rich Stadler and Denny Lombard, Lockheed Advanced Development Company; Eric Schulzinger, Lockheed Corporation; Tom Sprague, Teledyne Ryan Aeronautical; Robert F. Dorr; Peter M. Bowers; Harry S. Gann and Jim Ramsey, McDonnell Douglas Aerospace; Lois Lovisolo, Grumman Aerospace; Rick Kennedy, General Electric; Paul Oros, General Dynamics; historian Dr. Ira E. Chart, Northrop Corporation; Marty Isham; Gene Boswell and Erik Simonsen, Rockwell International Corporation, North American Aircraft; curator Doug Nelson, Air Force Flight Test Center Museum; Tony LeVier; John Guenther; Col. Harry C. Walker III; Robert K. Parsons (colonel USAF, retired); Fitzhugh L. "Fitz" Fulton Jr. (lieutenant colonel USAF, retired); Greg Field (special), Zack Miller, Tim Parker, and the rest of the editorial staff at Motorbooks International Publishers and Wholesalers.

Foreword

Immediately recognizing its remarkable potential for military aviation activities, then Lt. Col. Henry H. "Hap" Arnold selected a location on the western Mojave Desert as a bombing and gunnery training site for his March Field squadrons in 1933. Extremely isolated, Muroc Dry Lake—as it was then called—seemed ideal for his purposes. Its arid climate afforded excellent, year-round flying conditions and the enormous, flat, dry lake bed, sprawling out across 44sq-mi, would provide Arnold's aircrews with an airfield that could be maintained at no cost to the taxpayer. It was, in his words, "a natural aerodrome." General Arnold was, indeed, a man of vision, but he could not possibly have foreseen the remarkable events the future held for his remote bombing and gunnery range.

Muroc was changed forever on October 2, 1942, when the Bell XP-59A lifted off from the lake's northern edge, thus launching America's turbojet engine revolution. Though not a useful combat design, the Airacomet convincingly demonstrated radical new technology, and the successful conduct of its test program, without serious mishap, more or less settled the future of what was then called the Air Materiel Command Flight Test Base. Even though combat crew training would remain the dominant mission at Muroc's Main Base throughout the remainder of World War II, the volume of flight-test activity across the lake bed at North Base expanded in a crescendo of technology throughout these years, as all of the new jet airplanes and a host of other exotic air vehicles were wrung out in the skies overhead. Immediately after the war, the north and south base installations were merged and the full-time mission became flight test.

In the years since, the one-time remote bombing and gunnery range has evolved into one of the cornerstones of aerospace research and development, and it has become synonymous in the public mind with man's most daring achievements in flight. Indeed, throughout the postwar years, more major milestones in flight have taken place in the skies above Muroc-cum-Edwards than anywhere else in the world. Those skies became a unique, one-of-a-kind laboratory where men would dare to fly into unexplored regions—where, for the first time, they would pilot their aircraft past Mach 1, 2, 3, 4, 5, and 6, and up above 100, 200, and even 300,000ft and into near space. From Chuck Yeager's historic flight through the sonic "wall" to the majestic touchdown and rollout of the space shuttle *Columbia* after its fiery, Mach 25 re-entry from space, the event-filled history of Edwards Air Force Base offers a cornucopia of major breakthroughs. It has become famous, for example, as "the place where the rubber meets the ramp." More than 100 aircraft have completed their maiden flights at the base. Virtually every airplane to enter U.S. Air Force inventory over the past five decades has first passed through the ordeal of flight test in the skies over Edwards. A sizable number of U.S. Navy and U.S. Army air vehicles have blitzed these skies as well.

For five decades, the U.S. Air Force and, indeed, the world of aerospace have continued to meet their future in the skies above the sprawling expanse of the base. But this has been just a prelude. Edwards remains—and will continue to be— the place for those who want to explore the limits, and then go beyond.

Dr. James O. Young, March 1993
Chief Historian
Air Force Flight Test Center History Office
Edwards Air Force Base, California

Preface

When I initially discussed this work with Dr. James Young, chief historian for the Air Force Flight Test Center History Office, he stated, "It will be a daunting project." In essence, he said that it would be nearly impossible to cover more than a half-century of aviation history—especially an event-filled history such as that recorded at Edwards AFB—in a single volume.

Therefore, knowing that every recorded event at Edwards could not be documented in this work, I decided that only the most important historical occurrences would be discussed. But with so many significant events to consider, it became a question of what not to discuss. In other words, it was more difficult to determine which important events to eliminate than it was to decide which events to include. Those stories not told are no less important, and, without doubt, they will be discussed in future volumes.

Thus, with the limited space herein, an illustrated historical overview of Edwards Air Force Base follows. Though not a definitive work, this reference describes many dynamic advancements and aeronautical and astronautical events that have occurred at Edwards over the last five decades.

Welcome to Edwards Air Force Base.

Steve Pace, April 1994

Historical and Operational Overview

Edwards Air Force Base, located in California's Antelope Valley, is the premier flight-test and flight-research center in the world, with a proven record of accomplishments and contributions to the development of the aerospace sciences.

Edwards was the scene of supersonic breakthroughs from 1947 through 1967. On October 14, 1947, USAF Capt. Charles E. "Chuck" Yeager became the first pilot to exceed the speed of sound while flying the rocket-powered Bell X-1 research airplane from Muroc Army Air Field (as Edwards Air Force Base was then known). On October 3, 1967, almost exactly twenty years later, USAF Capt. William J. "Bill" Knight became "the fastest man alive" when he flew the rocket-powered North American X-15 to more than six-and-one-half times the speed of sound from Edwards AFB.

All of the postwar Century Series of USAF fighters, the F-100, F-101, F-102, F-104, F-105, F-106, F-107, F-110 (later redesignated F-4C), and the first practical swing-wing airplane, the F-111, were extensively tested at Edwards AFB during the 1950s and 1960s. The Lockheed C-5 Galaxy, North American's XB-70, and Lockheed's YF-12 and SR-71 were also tested there during the 1960s. Moreover, new generations of attack, bomber, fighter, and transport aircraft—the A-10, B-1, F-15 and F-16, and the YC-15—flew at Edwards during the 1970s. In total, more than 100 types of aircraft have made either their first flight or first landing at Edwards AFB.

Edwards AFB has also played a vital role in the nation's space program. The NASA space shuttle has utilized the Air Force Flight Test Center as its landing and ferrying site following missions in space. This use of the center follows a long tradition of space-related research undertaken at the base. In the 1960s, the rocket-powered X-15 research airplane operated on the fringes of space after being air-launched on missions from Edwards. The Air Force Rocket Propulsion Laboratory at Edwards developed and validated the design of rocket engines for the Apollo-Saturn V launch vehicle, which placed a total of twelve men on the moon. A group of wingless lifting bodies, culminating in the X-24B, demonstrated that these air vehicles could make powerless precision approaches and landings, helping to pave the way for the present-day space shuttles.

In January 1979, a major, new range and test facility known as the Utah Test and Training Range was activated under the Air Force Flight Test Center, managed by the USAF Materiel Command. The Utah Test and Training Range consolidated under single management the Hill and Wendover Air Force Test Ranges, a portion of the Dugway Proving Grounds, the airspace over Hill, Wendover, and Dugway ranges (restricted airspace), and adjoining military operating areas and air traffic control assigned airspace.

The Utah Test and Training Range has served as the test area for many unmanned aerospace air vehicles of various sizes and shapes at several locations since its formation. Unmanned aerospace vehicles tested at the Utah Test and Training Range were used in the Vietnam War, Israel, Operations Desert Shield and Desert Storm, and elsewhere. It was the prime test and training range for unmanned cruise missiles as well.

The Air Force Flight Test Center is tasked to support the USAF Materiel Command mission by conducting and supporting tests of manned and unmanned aerospace vehicles; conducting flight evaluation and recovery of research vehicles; performing development testing of an aerodynamic decelerator; operating the USAF Test Pilot School; developing, operating, and managing the Edwards Flight Test Range and the Utah Test and Training Range; supporting and participating in test and evaluation programs for the USAF, Defense Department, and other government agencies, as well as for airframe and powerplant contractors and foreign governments; and conducting flight tests for the deployment of nuclear weapons in support of the USAF Weapons Laboratory.

Edwards Flight Test Center is known for its ability to conduct aerodynamic tests such as performance and flying qualities evaluations. The capability to test and evaluate subsystems and to perform total weapons system evaluations has also existed since the mid-1950s. Total weapons system evaluations have been developed as a quantitative capability in the past ten to twelve years. Each subsystem is evaluated to determine whether it will perform as designed, whether it will perform its function in conjunction with other systems in a mission environment without interference, and its effects on the total system. Each weapons system is also evaluated under climatic extremes using the Climatic Laboratory at Eglin AFB in addition to arctic, desert, and tropical test sites. The reliability and maintainability of each subsystem, as well as the operational capability of the total weapons system, is assessed with eight phases (refer to Appendix B).

Additionally, the Flight Test Center performs development testing of mid-air retrieval systems for unmanned air vehicles. As part of the evolving capability to perform total weapons system evaluations, the Flight Test Center has developed the ability to conduct structural and flutter tests. A capacity to test and evaluate operational flight simulation trainers and to conduct the human factors evaluation likewise exists. The Flight Test Center also conducts research and development necessary for the improvement and modernization of ranges, facilities, and test techniques, as well as supporting the space shuttle program and evaluating its ability to support the Defense Department mission. Development of the capability to test and evaluate the atmospheric flight aspect of future manned air vehicles, such as the proposed National Aerospace Plane, is a continuing effort.

Edwards Flight Test Range is located on the western edge of the Mojave Desert, approximately 100mi north of Los Angeles, California, by highway. The range includes parts of San Bernardino, Kern, and Los Angeles Counties. Edwards Flight Test Range management's headquarters are located in the Ridley Mission Control Center at Edwards AFB. The location of Edwards AFB is vital to the accomplishment of its test and evaluation role in the aerospace industry. Natural attributes of the 470sq-mi (301,000 acres) base include its climate, terrain, weather, visibility, and sparse population. At an elevation of about 2,300ft, it has a typical desert climate and averages about 4in of rainfall per year. Edwards averages 345-plus sunny days per year, with low humidity and moderate temperatures the majority of the year.

A desert environment offers several natural assets that make Edwards a premier flight-test facility. Two dry lakes with beds of hardened clay are located on the base and serve as its marked and maintained runway areas. In addition, a number of off-base lake beds are used as both planned and emergency landing areas. Edwards' two primary lake beds are Rogers Dry Lake (formerly Muroc Dry Lake), which has about 60mi of marked and maintained runways on a dry lake bed that is about 12-1/2mi long and 5mi wide, and Rosamond Dry Lake, which has some 8mi of marked and maintained runways on a dry lake bed that is about 5mi long and 5mi wide. During the rainy season, these dry lakes occasionally become wet and retain water. In fact, it can even snow at Edwards, albeit rarely.

The western Mojave Desert has traditionally enjoyed excellent flying visibility—typically 10mi or more, 96 percent of the time—which is critical for photographic and video tracking, and remotely piloted vehicle operations.

The western desert area in which Edwards resides is sparsely populated, its relative remoteness making it an excellent area for flight-test activities. Special test areas, such as the mid- and high-altitude supersonic test and training corridors, are specifically located to have minimum impact on Edwards' neighbors.

Every major aircraft weapons system test effort for which the U.S. Air Force Flight Test Center is responsible is managed under the Combined Test Force or CTF concept. This test force is made up of representatives from the Edwards Flight Test Center, participating test organizations, the USAF Operational Test and Evaluation Center, both user and support commands, and contractors. The Combined Test Force is responsible for all aspects of planning; coordinating; managing; flight operations; safety; testing; reporting of development, test, and evaluation (DT&E) results; and for support of Initial Operational Test and Evaluation test programs. The B-52, B-1, B-2, C-17, F-15, F-16, F-22, and LANTIRN (Low Altitude Navigation and Targeting Infrared for Night) test programs at Edwards were all performed under Combined Test Forces.

The Air Force Flight Test Center test engineering and test capabilities include: propulsion, performance, flying qualities, fuel systems, environmental control systems, aircraft arresting systems, landing gear and brake systems, aircraft electrical and pneudraulic systems, human factors, manned aerospace air vehicles, unmanned aerospace air vehicles, reliability and maintainability, flight control systems, structural dynamics and flutter, avionics integration, weapons deliveries, aircraft aerial delivery by parachute, and all-weather/climatic tests.

Edwards Flight Test Range has the capability to receive real-time data and provide the mission control function of any mission being conducted along the 600-nautical-mile Southwest and Pacific West Coast test areas, from the Western Space and Missile Center to the Utah Test and Training Range, or to transfer the display and control to any other Defense Department range mission control center locations.

Ranges

Edwards has a number of weapons development ranges which together are called the Precision Impact Range Area (PIRA). These are critical to ongoing precision strike training for modern aircraft and ordnance.

The PIRA is divided into three ranges: West Range, East Range, and PB-6 Range. Each of these ranges can be scheduled individually or in conjunction with one another depending on mission requirements.

West Range

The West Range contains six precision bombing circles with scoring instrumentation and a dual air-to-ground gunnery range which is a conventional low-altitude air-to-ground gunnery, bombing, and rocket range with defined airspace. Each range consists of a bomb/rocket circle, ten strafe targets, two skip bomb targets, two flank observation towers, and a common range control tower.

East Range

The East Range contains one precision bombing circle and a five-target air-to-ground rocket range. This range is not instrumented with scoring limited to triangulation by use of transits. Future expansion is planned.

Hangar Complexes and Accessible Ranges

Edwards AFB has twenty aircraft hangar complexes, three with two hangar bays include office space for engineering and administrative personnel and shop and laboratory facilities. Thirteen hangars are located on Main Base, four at North Base (ideal for classified programs) and three at South Base. All thirteen Main Base hangars are adjacent to the main taxiways and connected to the 300ft by 15,000ft instrumented main runway with easy access to Rogers Dry Lake.

The four hangars at North Base are all located adjacent to taxiways that connect directly to both Rogers Dry Lake and a 150ft by 6,000ft asphalt runway; a parking apron for small aircraft is available. The total complex is a relatively self-contained air base with administrative and laboratory facilities and is located on Air Force Flight Test Center property 6mi north of the Main Base runway.

The hangars at South Base are adjacent to a parking apron and have access to the Main Base concrete runway and the Main Base facilities. Access to Rogers Dry Lake is also available, as is administrative, shop, and storage space.

Eleven ranges within 600 nautical miles of the Air Force Flight Test Center are accessible. These include: the Western Space and Missile Center, Pt. Mugu, Naval Weapons Center, and Utah Test and Training Range. These ranges have a variety of weather conditions, geography, topography, and terrain (including over water) to accommodate many test needs.

In short, Edwards Air Force Base, home of the Air Force Flight Test Center, is ideal for flight-test research and a multitude of other aerospace-related functions whether military or civilian. It has been that way for more than fifty years and, without doubt, will remain that way for many years to come.

Chapter 1

Edwards Takes Off

The 1940s

The roots of the present lie buried in the past.
—Carl Sagan

Pre-Flight

Archeological findings indicate that native Americans lived in the area now known as Edwards Air Force Base on a seasonal basis as early as 200 centuries ago.

The region was first investigated by Spanish explorers in the eighteenth century and by American frontiersmen, such as John C. Fremont, in the early nineteenth century. It was not until the railroad expanded into the western Mojave Desert in the 1870s that the first permanent settlements appeared.

The Southern Pacific Railroad was first into the region in 1876, when it extended its network

John K. "Jack" Northrop's original semi-flying-wing design, first flown at Muroc Dry Lake on September 26, 1929, was a move toward his first all-flying-wing design of 1939. Originally a pusher (rear-mounted propeller) with a single seat for its pilot, this twin-boom, twin-tail airplane was later modified to be a tractor (forward-mounted propeller) with two seats as shown. The Northrop B-2 Stealth bomber of today—the epitome of an all-flying-wing design—owes much to Northrop's early ventures into such air vehicles. Northrop

from the San Joaquin Valley in south central California, over the Tehachapi Mountains, down through the Antelope Valley in southeastern California toward Los Angeles. In 1882, additional tracks, which would ultimately become part of the Atchison, Topeka and Santa Fe network, were extended westward out of Barstow toward Mojave to cross the north shoreline of what is now Rogers Dry Lake on Edwards AFB.

A water stop was located at the northern edge of the giant dry lake, about 20mi southeast of Mojave, and in 1910, Clifford Corum, his wife, Effie, and his brother, Ralph, established a homestead nearby. Seeking to attract others to the area, they built a combination store and post office. Their request to have their business named Corum Mercantile Company was turned down by postal officials because a similar name was already in use elsewhere in California. Undaunted, they simply reversed the spelling of their last name to come up with the Muroc Mercantile Company. Muroc was a name that would stick in the region for almost four decades, the immense dry lake eventually carrying the name as well.

Muroc Dry Lake and the area east of it was first used by the U.S. Army Air Corps (USAAC) in September 1933, when a small detachment from March Army Air Field (now March Air Force Base) near Riverside, California, laid out the first of several temporary bombing and gunnery ranges. By May 1937, the entire USAAC was there conducting bombing and gunnery maneuvers, and a semi-permanent tent camp had been established along the lake bed's eastern shoreline. These USAAC personnel were first commanded by Lt. Col. Henry H. "Hap" Arnold, who became USAAC chief of staff and, later, U.S. Army Air Forces, chief of staff, before he became commanding general of the USAAF.

1940–1941

First designated the Muroc Bombing and Gunnery Range, then Muroc Army Air Field, and later Muroc Air Force Base, the once-fledgling base played an important role in the training of bomber and fighter crewmen throughout World War II. Beginning in December 1941, when it was established as a permanent training base, it became USAAC's primary World War II flight-test facility.

Very few flight-test activities came forth at Muroc during 1940 and through most of 1941, the exception being December 2, when the Curtiss CW-29B, a flying mock-up for the proposed Curtiss XP-55 Ascender, made its maiden flight after being transported by rail from Curtiss' Columbus, Ohio, facility.

Then, suddenly after the infamous attack on Pearl Harbor—in fact, during the afternoon of December 7—the newly established USAAF under the command of Lt. Gen. "Hap" Arnold opted to

This February 8, 1935, photograph shows the 73rd Pursuit Squadron's tent quarters at Muroc Gunnery Camp, as Edwards was then called. USAF via AFFTC/HO

employ Muroc in the defense of America's somewhat vulnerable West Coast. Just a few short weeks after Pearl Harbor, Muroc had been transformed from a small, obscure detachment of barely 100 men to a vital training center for thousands of aircrews and support personnel being prepared for war. Its isolated desert location and its typically clear skies made Muroc a very important training base.

To start, the USAAF moved its 41st Bombardment Group (BG) and its 6th Reconnaissance Squadron (RS) to Muroc to initiate bomber and reconnaissance crew training. Money was made available to build a concrete runway, a water sewage system, and numerous temporary structures, including barracks and hangars. On Christmas Eve 1941, the 30th BG and 2nd RS moved in.

1942

In July 1942, Col. Curtis E. LeMay arrived with his 305th BG. LeMay, who later became commander of the Strategic Air Command (October 19, 1948, to June 30, 1957), recalled that, at the time, "Muroc had no hangars and we were forced to do maintenance at night, when the planes had cooled off sufficiently to keep one from being burned on contact." While LeMay's 305th BG was at Muroc, he taught his aircrews the disciplined formation flying skills that would become the standard of the 8th Air Force over Western Europe during the war. The 305th BG flew Boeing B-17s. They were joined at Muroc by units flying Consolidated B-24s, North American B-25s, Martin B-26s, and Lockheed P-38s.

On July 24, USAAF Maj. Glenn L. Arbogast became the first commander of Muroc Army Air

A Martin B-12 twin-engine bomber from March Field (now March AFB) is serviced at Muroc Gunnery Camp on March 13, 1936. At the time, the B-12 was the US-AAC's premier bomber. USAF via AFFTC/HO

Field. In the 1940s, that amounted to responsibility for general air field operations. Arbogast commanded Muroc until December 12, 1942.

The most unusual site on Muroc Dry Lake during the early times was a full-scale, 650ft-long wooden mock-up of a Japanese Navy *Mogami*-class heavy cruiser. Christened the *Muroc Maru*, it was used for ship identification, strafing, and ship bombing practice by medium-class bomber crews flying B-25s and B-26s. The *Muroc Maru* helped new flyers and crews learn low-level skip-bombing and other tactics. Located at the dry lake's western edge, the phony ship—afloat in the shimmering heat waves radiating from Muroc Dry Lake—startled many motorists traveling along the northern edge of the base. The ship was not dismantled until 1950 when it was declared an on-base flight hazard.

In mid-1942, a USAAF team from the Air Materiel Command (now Air Force Materiel Com-

mand (AFMC)) at Wright Army Air Field (now Wright-Patterson Air Force Base), Dayton, Ohio, arrived at Muroc to evaluate it as a potential site for a test program whose secrecy would rival the Manhattan Project's development of the atomic bomb. Three primary factors were considered in their deliberations: proximity to railroad transportation, distance from populated areas, and the availability of a suitable takeoff and landing field. Muroc Army Air Field easily met all three requirements. The test program would involve the General Electric I-A, America's first turbojet engine, and the Bell XP-59A, America's first turbojet-powered airplane; it was called Secret Project MX-397.

While USAAF combat crews trained at the lake bed's southern end (now known as South Base), the top-secret MX-397 project was to be held on the opposite shore some 6mi north (now known as North Base) at a hastily constructed site with a single hangar and a marked but unpaved runway. At the time, at South Base, Muroc's first flight-test Basewas under construction with authority of the USAAF Air Materiel Command.

After the Bell XP-59A arrived by rail from Buffalo, New York, on September 19, it was moved to the new hangar on the northern shoreline of

Muroc Dry Lake; subsequently, it was reassembled and ground tested in preparation for flight. On October 1, after a series of low- and medium-speed taxi runs to test the airplane's brake, rudder, and other systems, the airplane skipped off the lake bed and was actually "flown" to an altitude of about 25ft. Although this was counted as the unofficial first flight, the official first flight was scheduled for the next day when Larry Bell (founder and president of Bell Aircraft) and other dignitaries would be present to witness the event. On October 2, Bell test pilot Robert M. "Bob" Stanley took the XP-59A up for its official maiden flights, and the jet age was underway in America. USAAF Col. Laurence C. "Bill" Craigie flew its third flight that day to become America's first military jet airplane pilot.

On December 13, USAAF Col. Frank D. Gore became the second base commander; he led until March 13, 1944.

1943

On January 9, 1943, the first Lockheed C-69 (forerunner of Lockheed's famed tri-tailed Constellation series), having completed its initial flight tests at Burbank, California, landed at Muroc for ongoing tests. Six days later, on January 15 , Convair test pilot Frank W. Davis made the first flight on the Convair XP-54 Swoose Goose. This was followed on April 18 with the first flight of the Bell YP-59A, the service-test version of the prototype XP-59A, now named Airacomet.

By late-1943, training and replacement aircrews began to dominate base activities as Muroc's main focus turned to training select fighter pilots and bomber crews for combat in the European and Pacific war theaters. By early-1944, more than fifty aircrews were passing their "final exams" at Muroc each month.

Despite the hectic training schedule, flight-test activities on new types of aircraft continued at Muroc. It was a time of hardship and uncertainty, and America needed new and better aircraft to survive.

The Northrop XP-56 Silver Bullet (also dubbed *Black Bullet*) made its maiden flight at Muroc on September 6 with Northrop test pilot John W. Myers at the controls. This airplane, part of Secret Project MX-14, was one of three contenders to answer a USAAF requirement for a speedy pursuit interceptor. The two others were the Convair XP-

The Curtiss model CW-29B, with its canard foreplane, was a flying mock-up for the Curtiss XP-55 Ascender which, when it later appeared, was similar but larger and heavier. The CW-29B was first flown at Muroc, then later delivered to NACA-Langley for wind-tunnel evaluations. Smithsonian Collection via AFFTC/HO

54 Swoose Goose and the Curtiss XP-55 Ascender, the latter making its first flight on July 19 at Scott Army Air Field near Curtiss' St. Louis, Missouri, plant. All three of these airplanes were deemed too troublesome, and none ever entered production.

Northrop test pilot John Myers again took to the skies on October 2, this time in the Northrop Rocket Wing. After being towed aloft behind a Lockheed P-38, the Rocket Wing made its first unpowered glide flight. The airplane, if successful under Secret Project MX-334, was to become the XP-79, a rocket-powered pursuit interceptor. It had been created from the third of three MX-324 unpowered glider air vehicles produced by Northrop. At the time, however, there were development delays on the aircraft's rocket motor, and powered flight-test activities did not occur until mid-1944. At least, the vehicle's airworthiness had been proved.

1944

USAAF Col. Robert O. Cork replaced Colonel Gore on March 14, 1944, on a temporary basis. Colonel Cork was replaced by Col. Ralph A. Snavely on April 1 (also a temporary assignment), and on May 1 Snavely was replaced by Col. Gerald E. Hoyle. These quick turnovers were the result of the growing war effort's need for group and squadron leaders.

One of the most successful of the early flight tests at Muroc occurred in early-1944 under Secret Project MX-409; this was the premier flight of Lockheed XP-80. Dubbed *Lulu-Belle*, this proto-

Left
Muroc Gunnery Camp's first commander "Hap" Arnold, who was commanding general of the USAAF when this photograph was taken, poses by his personal transport, a B-25C Mitchell, on the day he accepted it. Rockwell via Chris Wamsley

The all-wood Muroc Maru sails across Muroc Dry Lake while a lone B-25 makes a stern-to-bow strafing run on it. USAF via AFFTC/HO

Left
Lockheed's beautiful C-69 Constellation transport on a flight-test from Muroc AAF, circa 1943. The classic "Connie," recently celebrated its golden anniversary. Lockheed

Above
America's premier jet-powered airplane, the Bell XP-59A Airacomet, rests on Muroc Dry Lake following a successful flight test. Its wide-stance main landing gear is noteworthy. USAF via AFFTC/HO

The Consolidated Vultee Aircraft (later Convair) XP-54 Swoose Goose was a pusher design. Like Curtiss' XP-55 and Northrop's XP-56, it was never ordered into production. By the time these three pushers had flown, they had *been overtaken by the technologies they helped create. Ordered under Project MX-12, if produced, the production P-54 would have been armed with two .50-caliber machine guns and two 37mm cannons.* General Dynamics

type pursuit interceptor formed the matrix that defined the USAAF's first operational jet-powered fighter—the F-80 Shooting Star.

In preparation for the first flight, the airplane underwent a final engine run-up the evening before. Unfortunately, the XP-80's engine air inlet ducts collapsed, duct metal was sucked into the British-built de Havilland Goblin engine, and the engine—the only one in America—was destroyed. Lockheed replaced the XP-80's duct system while awaiting a replacement engine.

The new engine arrived in early-January 1944, and on January 8 Lockheed test pilot Milo Burcham lifted off the dry lake bed on the XP-80's maiden flight. It was a short hop, quickly followed by a longer flight in which he put *Lulu-Belle* through a number of precise maneuvers. Unlike the struggling Bell XP-59A, the XP-80 was an instant hit, and the USAAF wanted more and soon.

Next up for Muroc test trials was Bell's XP-77. Bell test pilot Jack Woolams was at the controls, ultimately pulling triple duty on the XP-77, XP-59A, and YP-59A programs when fellow Bell pilot

Bob Stanley was called back to Buffalo for other test pilot duties.

Lockheed's XP-58 Chain Lightning, flown by Lockheed test pilot Joe Towle on June 6, landed at Muroc following its maiden flight from Burbank. Following some twenty-five test hops at Muroc, the one-of-a-kind XP-58 was ferried to Wright AAF for ongoing evaluations.

Lockheed's XP-80A was also on hand at this time, being put through its paces by Lockheed test pilot Anthony W. "Tony" LeVier. Dubbed *Grey Ghost* because of its all-grey paint scheme, the XP-80A was a larger, more powerful version of the XP-80; its first flight occurred on June 10.

Another unique flight-test program came about in mid-1944 (no record of actual date). This involved another Northrop secret project (MX-543), this one dealing with the proposed JB-1 Bat, an unmanned, jet-powered bomb *a la* Germany's V-1 Buzz Bomb. Of twelve ordered, only two were built. The number one JB-1 was unpowered for aerodynamic evaluation with a pilot, and first flown by Northrop test pilot Harry Crosby. The powered (two 400lb-thrust General Electric B1 turbojets) JB-1 was guided with a pre-programmed guidance system. In late-1944, following cancellation of the remaining JB-1 order, the JB-1 airframe was redesigned and redesignated JB-10 under Secret Project MX-544. Thus, during 1945, ten JB-10s were tested at both Muroc AAF and Eglin AAF (now Eglin Air Force Base) in Florida. The JB-10s were unmanned and powered with two Ford PJ-31-1 turbojets (a Ford Motor Company version of the pulse-type jet engine used in German V-1s).

One of the most interesting airplanes tested in 1944 was Northrop's unique Rocket Wing (MX-334). After the installation of an interim 200lb-thrust rocket motor developed by Aerojet (the ultimate motor was to produce 2,000lb thrust), the Rocket Wing was prepared for powered flight-test activities. On July 5, after being towed aloft to 8,000ft behind a P-38 Lightning, Northrop test pilot Harry Crosby released the towline and fired the rocket motor. His four-minute flight was followed by a good landing on the lake bed. Thus, just twenty-one months after America had entered the jet age, it had entered the rocket age. It was a time of newer and bolder concepts that ultimately spawned a vast number of advanced aircraft and spacecraft—manned and unmanned—to lead America to the forefront of aviation.

Unpainted and gleaming in bare aluminum alloy, *Silver Ghost*, the second of two YP-80As, was flight tested at Muroc by Tony LeVier on August 1. With the combined successes of the XP-80 and XP-80As, the USAAF ordered service-test XP-80As that, after subsequent testing, led to the procurement of production P-80As for the war effort. However, the war ended before they could be put in service.

As 1944 drew to a close, Col. Warren E. Maxwell was appointed commander; he served until May 1, 1946.

1945

With the dawning of the jet age in America, a third new type of jet-powered fighter arrived on January 2, 1945. The Convair XP-81 was a com-

The sixth of thirteen service-test Bell YP-59A Airacomet airplanes as it appeared at Muroc in late-1943. Although P-59s were too slow and too unstable to make good gun-firing platforms, they moved America forward in the jet age. If it had not been for aircraft like this, today's USAF would not have such notable fighters as the F-15, F-16, and others. USAF via General Electric

posite-power-type airplane and was designed to fly with a tail-mounted General Electric gas turbine (turbojet) engine and a nose-mounted General Electric propeller-turbine (turbopropjet) engine. The goal with this powerplant arrangement was to give the XP-81 high speed and long range so that it could safely escort Boeing B-29s through Japanese airspace. On January 7, the first of two XP-81s made a successful first flight with Convair test pilot Frank Davis at its controls. However, since its design turbopropjet engine was not yet ready for flight, it made its first flight with a piston engine in the nose.

Flight-test activities continued with a number of different propeller-driven and jet-powered aircraft at Muroc through late-winter, spring, and early summer 1945. Late that summer, the Northrop XP-79B (built under Secret Project MX-365) arrived by truck. After a series of low- to medium-speed taxi runs over Muroc Dry Lake, it was ready for flight. On the morning of September 12, Northrop test pilot Harry Crosby rotated and took off in the one-of-a-kind XP-79B.

While piloting this flying-wing airplane from the prone position, Crosby executed a beautiful demonstration for some fifteen minutes. Suddenly, tragedy struck when the airplane entered what appeared to be a normal slow-roll maneuver from which it did not recover. Crosby attempted to bail out, but the air vehicle's speed was so high he was unable to clear it, and he was killed. The program was soon ended and no more P-79s were built. Crosby, America's premier rocketman and a respected test pilot, had paid the dearest price.

With the arrival of its design turbopropjet engine in late-1945, the number one XP-81 made a successful "second" first flight on December 21 with Frank Davis in control. Ultimately, this composite-power fighter did not demonstrate adequate performance, and the P-81 program was later terminated.

1946

In late-1945, the number one Republic XP-84, the USAAF's fourth jet-powered fighter, arrived by truck at Muroc AAF for its flight-test demonstrations. Forerunner of the famed Thunderjet series,

Ordered under Project MX-14, Northrop produced a pair of XP-56 prototypes for evaluation with Consolidated's XP-54 and Curtiss' XP-55. Unofficially dubbed Black Bullet *for obvious reasons, the XP-56 was of a semi-flying-wing design.* Northrop

20

The Curtiss XP-55 Ascender did not make its first flight at Muroc AAF. Of the three pusher-type aircraft tested (XP-54, XP-55, and XP-56), the XP-55 was the most fa- *vorable. Nevertheless, none of them entered production.* USAF via AFFTC/HO

the first of three XP-84s was successfully flown on February 28, 1946, by USAAF Maj. Wallace A. "Wally" Lien. This first flight and subsequent flights led to the production of many versions of one of Republic's most successful aircraft programs.

On May 2, 1946, Col. Signa A. Gilkey took command of Muroc AAF; he served until August 31, 1949.

On September 7, XP-84 number two, piloted by USAAF Capt. Martin L. Smith, set a new U.S. speed record of just over 611mph at Muroc. Smith's accomplishment, though impressive, was still some 5mph less than the official world speed record of 615.8mph established in England earlier that day by a Gloster F.4 Meteor. Nevertheless, in only four years, America had joined the world's elite in jet aviation.

Muroc AAF and its giant dry lake bed had become *the* place to flight test new aircraft. The U.S. Navy, having a flight-test facility of its own at Patuxent River, Maryland, was very aware of Muroc's flight-test facility. Thus, when North American suggested that the USN's newest jet fighter, the XFJ-1 Fury, be initially tested at

Muroc, the USN was all for it. Moreover, since North American was much closer to Muroc than Patuxent River, it would save travel time and cost over rail, truck, or ship transportation. So on September 12, with Maj. "Wally" Lien under glass, on loan from the USAAF, the first of three XFJ-1 Fury prototypes was successfully flight tested at Muroc.

Earlier, on May 17, America's first jet-powered bomber—the Douglas XB-43, a derivative of the Douglas XB-42 Mixmaster—was successfully flight tested at Muroc by Douglas test pilot Bob Brush and Douglas flight-test engineer Russ Thaw. A pair of XB-43s were built and flown, and though they proved to be aerodynamically stable, each was underpowered and the type was never ordered into production under Secret Project MX-475. The advent of the XB-43, however, set the wheels in motion that ultimately led to America's jet-powered bomber aircraft surpassing every nation on Earth.

The first of two Northrop XB-35 Flying Wing bombers took off on June 25, 1946, from Northrop's Hawthorne, California, facility and, af-

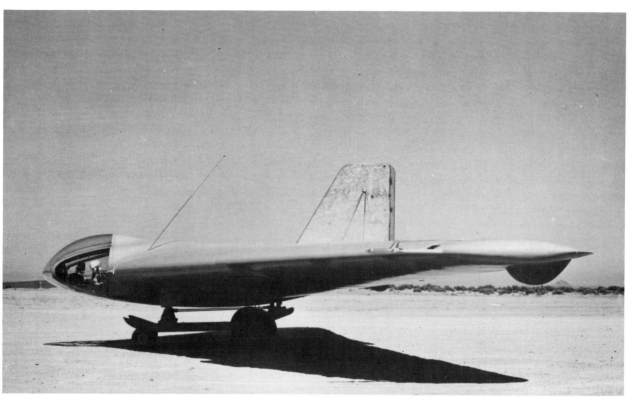

A Northrop MX-324 unpowered glider sits motionless on its takeoff wheels and landing skids. After rotation, the wheels dropped off so that the lightweight MX-324 could land on its skids; its pilot lay prone. Northrop

The third MX-324 was modified into the MX-334 Rocket Wing. Powered by an interim 200lb-thrust rocket motor, the proposed XP-79 interceptor was to have a 2000lb-thrust rocket motor. The MX-334 was the first manned rocket-powered airplane to fly in America. Northrop

Northrop JB-1 number one (shown) was the only piloted and unpowered JB-1 built, thus, it was used for aerody- *namic tests only. Unlike the pilot of the MX-324 and MX-334, the pilot of the JB-1 (MX-543) sat upright.* Northrop

ter a successful flying demonstration, landed at Muroc to undergo additional tests under Secret Project MX-140. The XB-35's competitor, the Convair XB-36, was first flown at Convair's Fort Worth, Texas, facility on August 8. It was then ferried to Muroc for further flight testing and evaluation against Northrop's Flying Wing. Ultimately, because of its greater speed, range, and stability as a bombardment platform, the XB-36 prevailed.

Flight-test activity was really heating up by summer 1946. Five NACA-Langley Research Center aerodynamics engineers arrived at Muroc from Langley, Virginia, to prepare for supersonic flight-test activities on the three Bell X-1 (formerly XS-1) rocket-powered air vehicles under a joint USAAF/ NACA program. The Langley engineers helped establish a temporary High Speed Flight Station at Muroc which, in 1947, became NACA's premier flight-test facility. It was later named NASA's Dryden Flight Research Facility in conjunction with NASA's Ames Research Center at NAS Moffett Field, California. Dr. Hugh L. Dryden of NACA-cum-NASA was responsible for setting up a permanent facility at Muroc in 1947;

hence, as its first director, it now carries his name.

On July 7, 1946, near Hughes Aircraft's Culver City, California, facility, the legendary Howard Hughes took off on the first flight of his sleek, prototype XF-11 photographic reconnaissance airplane. One hour and fifteen minutes later, due to a reverse pitch condition on the right-hand engine's rear propeller (the XF-11's two piston engines were each equipped with two contra-rotating propellers to help reduce torque), the airplane crashed and Hughes was seriously injured. Because of that mishap, the second of two XF-11s on order was trucked to Muroc for flight test. Later, on April 5, 1947, with a now-recovered Hughes at its controls, the number two XF-11 made a successful first flight at Muroc AAF.

The second USN jet fighter to be tested at Muroc AAF was the first of three Chance Vought XF6U-1 Pirate prototypes. On October 2, with Chance Vought test pilot Edward M. "Ted" Owens in control, the number one Pirate was successfully flown for twenty-four minutes before an engine accessory drive failed and forced a premature landing on the lake bed. This was Chance Vought's

America's second jet-powered airplane, the Lockheed XP-80 Shooting Star, sits on the Muroc AAF flight line waiting for yet another 500mph flight. With a single jet engine, Lulu-Belle, as it was nicknamed, totally out- *classed its twin-jet XP-59A predecessor. Note the original Muroc air traffic control tower in the background.* Lockheed

first jet-propelled fighter and forerunner to its famed Crusader series. On November 10, with Ryan test pilot Al Conover under glass, the one-of-a-kind XF2R-1 Dark Shark was successfully flown at Muroc. This composite-powered airplane had a turbojet in its tail and a turbopropjet in its nose. The Dark Shark was the first turbopropjet-powered airplane to fly in U.S. Navy dress.

On the following day, after being carried aloft by a B-29 mother ship, the number two Bell X-1 made its first glide flight at Muroc with Bell test pilot Chalmers H. "Slick" Goodlin in the cockpit. The number one X-1 had been grounded for a wing modification program after making ten earlier glide flights at Pinecastle AAF, Florida. This was the first flight of X-1 number two at either location.

Two days earlier, after departing Lockheed's Burbank facility, the first of two XR60-1 Constitution airplanes landed at Muroc after a successful

two-hour and seventeen-minute flight. The premier Constitution, forerunner of a proposed fleet of USN transports, was piloted by Lockheed's Joe Towle and copiloted by Tony LeVier. Ultimately, this program was canceled, and only the two prototype XR60-1s (redesignated XR6V-1s in 1950) were built.

With "Slick" Goodlin again at the controls, X-1 number two made its first powered flight on December 9 at Muroc. During the flight, 0.75 Mach

Right
Famed Lockheed test pilot Milo Burcham (left) (first to fly the XP-80 on January 8, 1944) discusses a new-type dive flap on the P-38 Lightning with the leading ace of World War II, USAAF Maj. Richard I. "Dick" Bong, circa late-1943. Bong, who died August 6, 1945, in the crash of a P-80A just after takeoff from Lockheed's Van Nuys, California, facility, had forty kills in WW-II. He also held a Medal of Honor. Lockheed

24

An experimental bomber escort and anti-shipping fighter, the Lockheed XP-58 Chain Lightning was one-third larger than the P-38. If produced, production P-58s were to carry twin tail turrets, each mounting two .50 caliber machine guns and four nose-mounted 37mm cannons, which would have been exchangeable for a nose section mounting a single 75mm cannon for special missions. Lockheed

Muroc AAF flight line activities on May 15, 1944, find a Consolidated B-24 Liberator being gassed prior to yet another bombing test on Muroc Dry Lake's eastern shore. USAF via AFFTC/HO

number (510mph) was attained at 35,000ft. Even though manned rocket flight had occurred earlier with Northrop's MX-334, this flight was the *real* precursor to the many fantastic rocket aircraft performance events that would follow.

1947

The first of three jet-powered XB-45 Tornado prototypes made a successful first flight on March 17, 1947. North American's George Krebs was pilot while Paul Brewer of North American served as copilot. The XB-45 was a quad-powered airplane with four turbojet engines (two on each wing), and,

ultimately, it became the first jet-powered bomber airplane to enter service with the USAAF-cum-USAF, but with much more powerful engines than those with which it was first tested.

On April 2, a second four-jet prototype bomber, the Convair XB-46, landed at Muroc after its first takeoff from Convair's San Diego, California, facility. Convair's Ellis D. "Sam" Shannon was pilot and Convair's Bill Martin was copilot.

The XB-46 was, to many, one of the most eye-pleasing aircraft ever built. Three XB-46s had been ordered, but only one was built and flown because Boeing's XB-47 Stratojet was to totally out-

A scaled-up version of the original XP-80, the XP-80A. It had a larger, heavier, and higher-thrust J33 turbojet which allowed it a 50mph faster top speed. Whereas the *XP-80 could hit 500mph, the XP-80A was capable of 550mph. Lockheed*

The one-of-a-kind Northrop XP-79B (MX-365) was created from the number three XP-79 airframe after the rocket-powered XP-79 interceptor was canceled; XP-79 airframes one and two were scrapped. Powered by two J30 turbojet engines, instead of a single 2,000lb-thrust rocket motor, the XP-79B was to be capable of similar performance. After crashing to destruction during its first flight, the XP-79B was likewise axed. USAF via AFFTC/HO

class the XB-46 and others with its own undeniable elegance. After early flight-test activities at Boeing's Seattle and Moses Lake, Washington, facilities, both XB-47 prototypes were ferried to Muroc AAF for ongoing tests in the late-1940s, the first XB-47 making its premier flight on December 17, 1947, the second on July 21, 1948.

As the USAAF and the NACA had already discovered, the U.S. Navy decided that Muroc AAF was a good place to pursue advanced performance for its airplanes. Thus, on April 15, with Douglas test pilot Eugene F. "Gene" May in control, the first of three Douglas D-558-1 Skystreak research air vehicles made a successful maiden flight. Powered by a single turbojet engine, the Navy's Skystreak was optimized to evaluate flight characteristics of an airplane in the transonic speed regime—that is, 600–800mph. And, although none of the three Sky-streaks ever attained 800mph (or even 700mph), one did establish an absolute world speed record (to be discussed later in the text).

One of two XB-42s retrofitted with a turbojet engine under either wing in addition to its two tail-mounted piston-powered, propeller-driven engines, was initially flight tested at Muroc by pilots Bob

With one turning and one burning, the composite-powered Consolidated XP-81 was essentially a push-me/pull-me airplane. The number two XP-81 is shown taxiing out for a flight test, circa late-1945. USAF via AFFTC/HO

Brush and Russell J. "Russ" Thaw on May 27. This modified airplane was designated XB-42A. The XB-42 was first flown at Douglas' Santa Monica, California, facility on May 6, 1944, with Douglas pilots Brush and Thaw at its controls. The proposed B-42A was never ordered into production. The one-of-a-kind XB-42A was used subsequently as a turbojet engine test bed for various makes and models. In the end, the XB-42, XB-42A, and XB-43 aircraft became aviation history footnotes.

With all this flight-test activity, Muroc AAF was the site of numerous aviation speed and altitude records. One such record was established June 19, when USAAF Col. Albert Boyd, then flight-test division chief of the Air Technical Service Command (ATSC) at Wright AAF, averaged 623.738mph over Muroc Dry Lake at low altitude. To do this, he piloted a modified Lockheed XP-80B, redesignated XP-80R (for *Racey*), powered by a single Allison Model 400 (a modified Allison-built

General Electric J33 turbojet with a water and methanol injection system). Boyd's run returned the world's absolute speed record to the United States for the first time in many years. As it turned out, Colonel Boyd's speed record was just the beginning.

It was during the late-1940s that American-built, turbojet-powered aircraft began to make their presence known throughout the world. The USAAF's fresh world speed record of 623-plus mph on paper, gave the USN impetus to try rewriting the record books with its number one Douglas D-558-1 Skystreak.

The Navy realized its goal on August 20 when USN Cdr. Turner F. Caldwell Jr. brought the U.S. Navy its first world speed record in nearly a quarter of a century. After taking off at 8:28 a.m., Caldwell made four required speed runs at about 75ft above a special speed course at Muroc AAF. At the end of his 90mi, some sixteen-minute flight above

The Republic XP-84 Thunderjet, powered by a single jet engine of axial-flow design, was the USAF's first 600mph fighter plane. Shown is XP-84 number one on the ramp at North Base, circa 1946. USAF via AFFTC/HO

Muroc Dry Lake, the Annapolis-bred flier had established a new absolute world speed record of an averaged 640.663mph or 0.82 Mach number. Caldwell's blast over the sanctioned 3km course erased USAAF Colonel Boyd's two-month-old mark by some 17mph.

Five days later, Commander Caldwell's brand-new record was erased using the very same plane. On August 25, U.S. Marine Corps Major and World War II fighter ace Marion E. Carl raised the record to an average speed of 650.606mph during four passes over the course at Muroc AAF. It should be noted that this plane, and its engine, came "factory stock" without any special modifications. So, in eighteen months' time, one U.S. and three world speed records had been established at Muroc AAF.

On September 18, the U.S. Army Air Force was disestablished and, in its place, effective September 26, the whole and separate U.S. Air Force (USAF) was established under the command of Gen. Carl A. Spaatz. He served as USAF chief of staff until his retirement April 29, 1948.

On October 1, the first of three sweptback-winged XP-86 Sabre prototypes made a successful first flight with North American's George S. "Wheaties" Welch at the controls.

Even more momentous was USAF Capt. Charles E. "Chuck" Yeager's October 14 flight of the number one Bell X-1. After being dropped from the belly of its B-29 mother ship, the X-1 hit 1.06 Mach number (700mph) at about 42,000ft above Muroc Dry Lake. For the first time in history, the speed of sound had been surpassed by a manned air vehicle—the so-called supersonic wall had been penetrated.

Although there is no documentation to prove it, there is a movement to try and prove that George

The first of three North American XFJ-1 Fury prototypes flies above Muroc Dry Lake on its maiden flight with USAAF Maj. "Wally" Lien under glass. Lien, on loan to North American for the event (qualified contractor jet airplane pilots were scarce at the time), had made the

first flight of Republic's XP-84 earlier. Originally, North American's XP-86 Sabre was similar to the XFJ-1. However, with USAAF approval, it was redesigned with aftward-swept flying surfaces. The result: The Sabre, with the same engine, was nearly 100mph faster! Rockwell

Welch might have exceeded the speed of sound before Chuck Yeager. It is contended that this occurred during a dive from 30,000ft in the number one XP-86 during its early flight-test activities between October 1 and 14, 1947. Although the Welch claim has yet to be substantiated, it is a fact that XP-86s did indeed surpass the speed of sound in dives from high altitude during their many test flights over Muroc Dry Lake. The author, who was lucky enough to meet Brigadier General Yeager on

October 2, 1992—the fiftieth anniversary of the XP-59A's first official flight—wonders why such a move is on and why anyone would want to discredit this famed test pilot and patriot.

On October 21, after taking off at Hawthorne, the first of two jet-powered Northrop YB-49 Flying Wing bombers flew a successful test flight and landed at Muroc AFB for additional evaluation. This was followed in early-January 1948 by the number two Flying Wing.

An aerial view of the Main Base complex at Muroc AAF as it appeared on October 10, 1946. From this view, *Muroc's growth over the previous ten years or so is quite apparent.* USAF via AFFTC/HO

An aerial view of the North Base area of Muroc AAF as it appeared on October 10, 1946. To this day, North Base (called Muroc Flight Test Base when this photograph was taken) is still a restricted area and cannot be visited without special clearance. USAF via AFFTC/HO

On December 10, the first of three Douglas D-558-2 Skyrocket aircraft arrived at Muroc by truck. The D-558-2 was a sweptback-winged and -tailed version of the D-558-1 Skystreak, and ultimately, the first airplane on Earth to fly twice the speed of sound.

1948

Nineteen forty-eight started out busy and promising. Douglas test pilot John F. "Johnny" Martin made a successful first flight in the number one D-558-2 Skyrocket on February 4, 1948. One month later, on March 5, the one-and-only Curtiss XP-87 Blackhawk, a prototype for a proposed USAF jet-powered night and limited all-weather fighter, made its first flight at Muroc after being trucked-in from Curtiss' Columbus, Ohio, facility. It was piloted by Curtiss test pilot Lee Miller.

Developed under Project MX-475, the Douglas XB-43 twin-jet bomber prototype has the distinction of being America's first jet-powered bomber airplane. Proposed as a high-speed light bomber, production B-43s were to carry up to 4,000lb of bombs. The first of two XB-43s was grounded after a landing mishap February 1, 1951. Its parts were used to keep XB-43 number two flying; it was retired in late-1953. On October 30, 1953, it was ferried to Bolling Field where it was turned over to the National Air and Space Museum. McDonnell Douglas

"Jack" Northrop's dream of creating an all-flying wing came to fruition with the prototype XB-35 Flying Wing bomber. Developed under Project MX-140 to compete head-to-head with Consolidated's XB-36, the XB-35 proved to be an unstable bombardment platform, and the XB-36 prevailed. Yet, if not for the XB-35 of 1946 and its stablemate YB-49 of 1947, the B-2 would not exist. USAF via AFFTC/HO

Four model N-9Ms were built and flown by Northrop and the USAAF to serve as flying mockups for the XB-35 program. In all, according to a statement made by "Jack" Northrop, the four N-9Ms logged more than 200 flights during the early-1940s at Muroc AAF. USAF via AFFTC/HO

The World War II-era Consolidated XB-36 six-engine pusher prototype was the epitome of a heavy bombardment airplane—the essence of what such a bomber should be. After it had won the fly-off against the Northrop XB-35, the XB-36 was redesigned to become the B-36 Peacemaker, the Strategic Air Command's heaviest payload carrier until the arrival of the eight-jet Boeing B-52 Stratojet in 1955. General Dynamics

Although it was underpowered and ungainly, the Chance Vought Aircraft XF6U-1 Pirate was a learning tool that led to CVA's F8U (later F-8) Crusader—the Navy's first carrier-based supersonic fighter. Ling-Temco-Vought

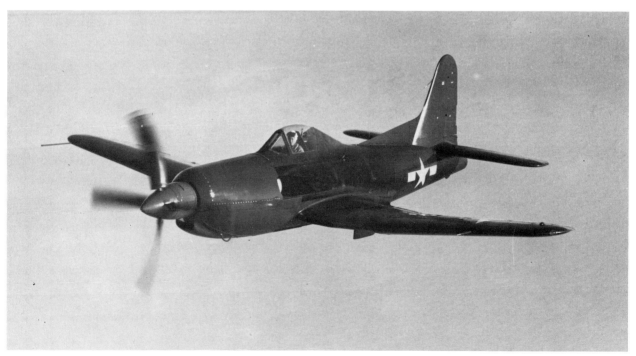

A composite-powered fighter prototype, the Ryan XFR2-1 Dark Shark had a turbopropjet in the nose and a turbojet in the tail. This is the only example that was built, as the FR2-1 program was terminated shortly after this plane's first flight. Teledyne Ryan Aeronautical

Success quickly turned to tragedy in May. In just over one month, Muroc AFB experienced two tragic airplane crashes that killed six men. The first of these, on May 3, happened to NACA pilot Howard C. Lilly while flying D-558-1 number two. It was the forty-sixth test flight of this particular Skystreak, during which the jet engine's compressor disintegrated and ripped the airplane in two. The airplane did not have an emergency ejection seat, and Lilly was not able to get out of the fast-moving and quickly disintegrating airplane.

The second tragedy occurred on June 5, slightly northwest of Muroc AFB and involved YB-49 number two. Believed to be caused by overstressing the airplane, the YB-49 disintegrated during flight, and all five crewmen aboard, including its copilot USAF Capt. Glen W. Edwards, perished.

A change in nomenclature took place June 10 when the Department of Defense ordered that P for Pursuit be changed to F for Fighter. Thus, beginning on June 11, the XP-86 became the XF-86, the TP-80C became the TF-80C, and so on.

In early-August 1948, Northrop trucked its prototype XF-89 Scorpion to Muroc from Hawthorne. On August 16, with Northrop test pilot Fred C. Bretcher at its controls, this proposed all-weather fighter-interceptor was successfully flight tested.

One week later, on August 23, the second of two McDonnell XF-85 Goblin prototypes (the first example had been damaged during a ground test) was taken aloft beneath its Boeing EB-29B mother ship *Monstro* for its first free flight over Muroc Dry Lake. The Goblin was a proposed Parasite Fighter and was really little more than a winged jet engine with a cockpit. It had already undergone a number of successful captive flights. With McDonnell test pilot Edwin F. "Ed" Schoch in control, XF-85 num-

To meet the USN's growing need for a heavy-lift land-based transport, Lockheed produced a pair of prototype XR60-1 Constitutions per USN contract authority. Although the R60-1 program was later canceled, the two prototypes were delivered to VR-44 (a USN transport squadron based at Naval Air Station, Alameda, California) in 1949. They remained in service until 1953. In 1955, they were sold as surplus for a mere $98,000. Number one is shown. Lockheed

ber two did make a successful flying demonstration after it was dropped from its mother ship. However, in the second attempt to dock with the B-29's trapeze, the trapeze's bridle hit the upper part of the cockpit canopy. The canopy shattered, and the bridle knocked Schoch's helmet and oxygen mask off, shocking him temporarily. He regained control of the airplane and made an emergency landing on the lake bed.

Although many flight-test programs at Muroc proved that many different mission concepts were valid, others proved to be invalid. This was the case for the Parasite Fighter program, which was canceled after only two hours and nineteen minutes of free flight between the two XF-85s. The USAF's revised Parasite Fighter program called FiCon for *Fighter Conveyor* fared a good deal better, but it, too, was short-lived.

On September 18, Convair test pilot "Sam" Shannon made a good first flight with the delta-wing Convair XF-92A Dart. This flight was historic because it was the world's first flight of a delta-winged air vehicle and the first flight of an airplane without a horizontal tailplane.

To answer the USAF's Penetration Fighter program both McDonnell and Lockheed had received contracts in 1946 to build and fly two prototypes. The former designated XF-88 and the latter designated XF-90 (formerly XP-88 and XP-90). The XF-88 was first to arrive at Muroc for flight test and evaluation. On October 20, 1948, with McDonnell test pilot Robert M. "Bob" Edholm under glass, the first of two XF-88 Voodoos made its first flight at Muroc. Its sister ship, was not flown until April 26, 1949, at Lambert Field, St. Louis, Missouri, and was subsequently ferried to Muroc for additional tests.

continued on page 42

The first of three North American prototype XB-45 four-jet bomber planes—forerunner of the USAF's fleet of B-45s, America's first operational jet-powered bomber—fuels-up with JP-1 (Jet Petroleum One) prior to its maiden *flight at Muroc Flight Test Base (now North Base). The hangar was relatively new at the time of this photograph. Rockwell via Chris Wamsley*

Anthony W. "Tony" LeVier

Tony LeVier, with more than 10,000 flying hours in more than 260 different types of aircraft, is one of America's most renowned test pilots. He served with Lockheed thirty-three years before retiring April 29, 1974. Among his lengthy list of "firsts," he was first to fly the following planes: the XF-90, the YF-94, the XF-104, and the U-2. He holds many awards and aviation-related memberships and is a living member of the Aviation Hall of Fame. He is currently the president of S.A.F.E. Inc. (Safe Action in Flight Emergency), which he founded.

"It was early one morning in April 1950 that I first flew faster than sound. I was at 40,000ft over the great Mojave Desert in Southern California on a test flight in a new swept-wing fighter plane, the Lockheed F-90, which was one of the first planes built to penetrate the sound barrier. For nearly a year, we had been testing this new airplane, since the first time I took it off the ground [for the official first flight on June 4, 1949], and now the time had come to find out how fast it would fly. That was my assignment this morning.

"I gave my instruments a final check, tightened my shoulder harness again for the last time, and turned west. Above me the desert sky was a bowl of dark blue, and before me the California mountains stretched hundreds of miles north and south. Fifty miles ahead and below I could see Edwards Air Force Base, the U.S. Air Force's great test center on the edge of the famous Muroc [now Rogers] Dry Lake, where I had flown so many times in other new jets.

"Up to now, not many men—or airplanes—had broken through the sound barrier. The 90 was a big plane for one man, weighing over 26,000lb, and it had two jet engines to enable it to climb very high and fly very fast. It was designed for supersonic speeds, and today we wanted to find out if it would stand up to the test. The only way to do that was to dive it through the sound barrier.

Tony LeVier (left)—truly a pilot's pilot—poses with Lockheed test pilot Herm Salmon beside a Lockheed YF-104A Starfighter, circa mid-1955. Salmon died June 22, 1980, in the crash of his privately owned Lockheed Model 1049 Constellation. *Lockheed*

"The plane was thoroughly instrumented. Up in front was an automatic observer, a motion picture camera of special design which automatically photographed an instrument panel in the nose of the plane. I also carried an oscillograph, an instrument connected to the various critical points of the airframe to record the stresses on the structure. In addition, I had an audiograph to record my comments and an open microphone to the ground. We were taking no chance on missing anything that happened, as many thousands of dollars had been spent in preparation for this flight, and to miss the smallest incident could not only cost a great deal of money but possibly my life on some future flight.

"On preliminary dives earlier in our test program, I had encountered a severe and alarming control problem on the 90, caused by the elevators seizing up and making it virtually impossible to move the [control] stick and change the flight path of the airplane. At high speeds, the air pressure on the elevators was ten to twenty times greater than normal. We overcame this condition by installing a hydraulic power boost for the controls to aid in maneuvering the airplane during high-speed flight.

"I had also been bothered by the adjustable [horizontal] stabilizer which was used on the 90 to trim the airplane in flight. Unlike the elevators, it was too sensitive and caused overcontrolling, making the [nose of the] plane pitch up and down quite sharply, much like a roller coaster, only more abrupt. I had also run into compressibility, the sudden change in air pressure at high speeds that can transform a normal airplane into a beast. But the 90 was not a beast, and compressibility never bothered this plane unduly, although it affects all planes and the problem certainly was there.

"The new hydraulic boost and the adjustable stabilizer had been tested on previous flights and everything should have been satisfactory. I was all squared off now, pulling top rpm in my engines with both afterburners going, and was rapidly approaching maximum level flight speed, which at 40,000ft was around 600mph. I was in constant radio communication with the engineers on the ground, giving them my position. East of North Base at Muroc [now Edwards], I told them to stand by for my dive.

"The method I always used in dive testing was to push forward on the stick and drop the nose without rolling the airplane. I arrived at the conclusion over years of testing that this method is probably the best from the standpoint of reaching the greatest [initial] speed. However, pushing over is an extremely uncomfortable maneuver, and one must be buckled in his seat very firmly and have his shoulder harness pulled tight to the point where it hurts.

"I pushed over at 0g, where my body was weightless and also the airplane, a maneuver considered to be the best for getting into a steep [nose-down] angle for a dive because it creates the least amount of drag. I was attempting to reach a 60deg angle within a space of 2,000 or 3,000ft. Normally, flying through the air at constant altitude, the plane and the pilot are pressing

downward at 1g, or equivalent to their own weight. By suddenly changing the path of the airplane downward equal to 1g, or the pull of gravity, weight vanishes.

"Everything appeared to be normal. All instruments checked okay. I trimmed my stabilizer for a nose-down condition and also to hold my dive at a very steep angle. As I got closer and closer to the magic number of Mach 1, I experienced all the little peculiar characteristics that take place in the transonic zone [600–800mph]. I noticed the tendency of the wing to drop, the sudden tucking and pitching, and the sudden action of the rudder as it trembled and kicked over several degrees. All this I was experiencing and talking over my hot mike [open microphone to the ground], explaining these behaviors of the aircraft and telling our [Lockheed's] ground crew my sensations as I rushed down faster and steeper.

"As I approached the sound barrier, it seemed a thousand hands were pulling back on the airplane, as if it were reaching a wall that was impenetrable. Then, suddenly, something released, and the airplane shot ahead. It is true, there is a wall there—a wall of tremendous drag—but once you have reached the speed of sound and the compressibility effects are stabilized, drag suddenly changes, and the airplane slips on ahead as though it were on a greased platter. The sound level even changes. The air rushing over the airplane and the roar of the engines behind you all add up to make noise, but as the speed of sound is exceeded this noise no longer can reach you, and you are ahead of this noise, traveling faster than sound. This sudden change in the sound level was one way I knew I had gone through the barrier.

"As I passed it, my Mach indicator stood at 1, and I said over the radio, 'There she is.' My speed was near 800mph and altitude about 27,000ft. Now it was time to pull out of the dive.

"From force of habit I pulled back on the stick but to no avail; it might just as well have been anchored in concrete. I immediately actuated the stabilizer switch on top of the pilot's stick grip to raise the nose of the airplane and effect recovery from the dive. Ordinarily the stabilizer would react almost instantly and the nose would start rising, but this time nothing happened.

"For several moments of bewilderment I sat motionless in the cockpit, with no apparent movement of change in the plane's attitude, watching the ground rush up to meet me at a 1,000ft per second. I could see North Base, the large expanse of dry lake bed where I had taken off only minutes before. The hangars along the edge of the lake and the ramp with other experimental aircraft ready for testing were in plain view. Startled and frightened, I had even stopped talking, and the engineers sitting in the radio room heard nothing but the sound of my heavy and rapid breathing over the radio.

"I was about to resort to the emergency stabilizer actuator and dive recovery flaps when I noticed the nose, ever so slightly, begin to rise. Then with the same abruptness with which it had burst beyond the

continued on next page

sonic barrier, the airplane came back through again. All the same weird characteristics were evident once more, but now the Mach number was dropping so rapidly they appeared as sharp jolts, such as are experienced when flying through extremely turbulent air.

"By this time I was only 20,000ft from the ground, and now the 90 was being subjected to air loads four times greater than at the beginning of the dive, where the air was much thinner. My indicated air speed was well over 500mph, which produces an impact pressure of about 650lb per square foot. It was this combination of tremendous forces and the high gs reacting on the 90 in its dive recovery that would have caused most airplanes to disintegrate. Now it was being put to its crucial test. Bucking like an untamed bronco, it plunged earthward, and then suddenly it was in level flight and still in one piece.

"As I flashed down toward the ground, I entered a haze level around 20,000ft, and the crew on the ground lost me from view. After what seemed a matter of seconds they heard two tremendous explosions in rapid succession, and off in the distance across the dry lake bed there rose a large cloud of dust from the desert floor. Jim White [a friend of LeVier's and a Lockheed test pilot] exclaimed, 'My God, he dove in!' Kelly Johnson [Lockheed chief research engineer and primary designer of the airplane] almost went to his knees and turned and ran into the hangar.

"It was quite obvious to them I had crashed. Two explosions and a cloud of dust—what else could it be? But by the time they had gotten to the radio. I reported pullout had just been made and everything was okay.

"The explosions they heard were sonic booms. No one at Muroc that day had ever heard it before. It is a sound that no one will ever get used to, for it is too tremendous and jolting.

"The cloud of dust the ground crew saw when they heard my 'booms' was one of those freak coincidences that had nothing to do with me. That same morning the Air Force was conducting practice bombing at a nearby bombing range. Apparently a bomber dropped a dummy bomb at the same time I made my dive. It hit 6 or 7mi from the ground crew, and it raised a dust cloud that could easily be thrown up by an airplane crashing at high speed into the desert floor.

"We also learned why I had trouble pulling out of my dive. The stabilizer turned out to be responding only 10 percent as fast as normal. In correcting the sensitivity I had complained of earlier, the engineers had rewound the armature in the electric motor to reduce its speed, which of course reduced its power. These are some of the little mistakes that can catch up with you and sometimes cause you trouble."

Excerpted with the permission of Tony LeVier and John Guenther from *Pilot*, first published by Harper and Brothers in 1954, and again in December 1990 by Bantam Books, New York, NY.

Author's note: By May 17, 1950, LeVier had dived the F-90 through the speed of sound a total of fifteen times, 1.12 Mach number being his best.

LeVier with the Lockheed XF104.

Regarded by many as one of the most elegant-looking air vehicles ever built and flown, the Consolidated XB-46 could not match the Boeing XB-47. Streamlined to near perfection, the XB-46's top speed of 545mph was too slow; thus, the 600mph XB-47 advanced. USAF via AFFTC/HO

continued from page 37

As 1948 drew to a close, the number two Douglas D-558-2 Skyrocket arrived at Muroc. Douglas test pilot Gene May made its successful first flight on November 2, 1948; it was delivered to NACA on December1.

Fifteen days later, on December 16, Northrop test pilot Charles Tucker made a successful first flight on the Northrop X-4 Bantam, the first of two semi-tailess research aircraft, under the USAF's Skylancer program known as project MX-810.

1949

Under Secret Project MX-909, Republic Aircraft produced two XF-91 Thunderceptor aircraft for flight-test activities at Muroc AFB. And on May 9, 1949, with Republic test pilot Carl A. Bellinger at the controls, the first example made its maiden flight over the dry lake bed.

The second Penetration Fighter contender, the Lockheed XF-90, arrived at Muroc in late-May 1949. On June 4, some eight months after the XF-88 had flown, Tony LeVier made the official first flight on the first of two XF-90s.

On June 7, in the hands of Northrop's Charles Tucker, the number two X-4 made its first flight; it would fly another 101 times with five USAF pilots and seven NACA pilots in addition to Tucker before the program's end.

On September 7, USAF Brig. Gen. Albert Boyd became base commander. General Boyd had flown earlier at Muroc in the XP-80R dubbed *Racey.* He was base commander until January 28, 1952.

On December 8, Muroc AFB was renamed Edwards AFB to honor USAF Capt. Glen W. Edwards, who died June 5 in the crash of YB-49 number two during a test hop.

As the sweptback-winged XP-86 became the class of all fighters in 1947, so did the sweptback-winged Boeing XB-47 Stratojet become the class of all bombers. Elegant from any angle, the XB-47 outclassed anything else in the air. Sporting six turbojet engines, and a top speed of more than 600mph, the Stratojet was an instant success. The first of two XB-47s is shown. Boeing

Three noted Douglas D-558-1 Skystreak test pilots— USMC Maj. Marion Carl (left), Douglas' Gene May (center), and USN Cmdr. Turner Caldwell—ham it up in *front of Skystreak number one on Muroc Dry Lake, circa mid-1947.* McDonnell Douglas via Harry Gann

The 1940s at Edwards AFB closed out for the most part on December 22, when, with North American's George Welch at the controls, the first of two North American YF-86D (formerly YF-95A) fighter-interceptor service-test aircraft made its successful first flight. This was a nighttime version of the daytime F-86 which looked different—so different in fact, it was redesignated F-95. Later, however, similarities outweighed dissimilarities and the F-95 became the D model of the F-86 Sabre series.

The 1940s had been an exciting decade at Muroc-cum-Edwards, with many dynamic plans put into practice and the vast aeronautical genius of America maturing dramatically. Of the many aircraft types originally tested at Edwards in the 1940s, ten military versions went into either limited- or full-scale production for the U.S. armed forces. These included:

- The Bell P-59 Airacomet (limited scale)
- The Lockheed F-80 Shooting Star (full scale)
- The Republic F-84 Thunderjet (full scale)
- The North American FJ-1 Fury (limited scale)
- The Chance Vought F6U-1 Pirate (limited scale)
- The North American B-45 Tornado (limited scale)
- The North American F-86 Sabre and F-86D Sabre Dog (full scale)
- The Lockheed T-33 T-Bird (full scale)
- The Northrop F-89 Scorpion (full scale)

From what had only been a desolate desert outpost some ten years earlier, Muroc had metamorphosed into a working flight-test center with more and more modern facilities and conveniences for its ever-increasing populations of military, government and civilian personnel. What would the 1950s bring?

After the crash of XF-11 number one, Howard Hughes decided it would be more prudent to flight test XF-11 number two at Muroc AAF instead of locally at Culver City. Now turning single, four-bladed propellers instead of dual, four-bladed propellers, the second XF-11 (shown) made a successful first flight at Muroc on April 5, 1947. The airplane was redesignated XR-11 in July 1948. AFFTC/HO via Tony Landis

Dubbed Flying Stove Pipe, *the Douglas D-558-1 Skystreak was the first jet-powered USN airplane to earn absolute world speed records: 640.663mph and 650.796mph. Both records were set during four passes* over a low-altitude, 3km (about 1.86mi) course at Muroc AAF. The first of three Skystreaks is shown with Douglas test pilot "Gene" May (right) and USN project pilot Cdr. Turner Caldwell. AFFTC/HO via Tony Landis

After USAAF cancellation of the Douglas XB-42 Mix-master light bomber program, a decision was made to experiment with XB-42 number two by installing a tur-bojet engine beneath each wing. So configured, it was re-designated XB-42A. Now powered by two 1,375hp Alli-son water-cooled piston engines and two 1,600lb-thrust Westinghouse axial-flow turbojet engines, the hybrid XB-42A was extensively tested at Muroc. AFFTC/HO via Tony Landis

Left
Col. Albert Boyd, then chief of the flight-test division of the USAAF Air Materiel Command, poses at the right-hand wing tip of Racey, the Lockheed XP-80R that he flew on June 19, 1947, to establish an absolute world speed record of 623.738mph. The XP-80R (formerly the ninth production P-80A, later modified to serve as the prototype XP-80B) was powered by a water- and methanol-injected 4,600lb-thrust Allison model 400 tur-bojet engine (a modified General Electric-designed, Alli-son-built J33). Colonel Boyd later became commander of Muroc AAF-cum-Edwards AFB. Lockheed

North American test pilot George Welch looks at the camera while flying the first of three XP-86 Sabre prototypes at Muroc in late-1947. The amazing F-86 would later see combat in the Korean War; by war's end, it had created thirty-nine USAF jet aces with five or more kills to their credit. Have you ever heard the phrase "You've been eighty-sixed"? The Sabre might have coined it . . . Rockwell via Chris Wamsley

The first of three first-generation Bell X-1 rocket-pow-ered aircraft—the very one with which Chuck Yeager first broke the speed of sound—is shown during an early powered flight-test over Muroc-cum-Rogers Dry Lake. Before its retirement, X-1 number one attained a best speed of 1.45 Mach number (957mph) on March 26, *1948. It was flown by Yeager, naturally! It was pho-tographed by chase pilot Bob Hoover from a Lockheed RF-80. The oil streak on the X-1's left outboard wing came from the B-29 launch plane's left inboard engine.*USAF via AFFTC/HO and Tony Landis

Forerunner of the Northrop B-2 Stealth bomber, the first of two Northrop YB-49 service-test flying wing bombers takes off at Muroc AAF in late-1947. Spanning 172ft (identical to the B-2), the YB-49 was underpowered by eight 3,750lb-thrust turbojet engines; its top speed was 493mph at 20,800ft. This YB-49 was scrapped after it crashed during a high-speed taxi test at Edwards AFB in March 1950. Northrop

The first of three Douglas D-558-2 Skyrocket research aircraft during a medium-speed taxi test on Muroc Dry Lake prior to its first flight. Originally designed for Mach one speed, the Skyrocket ultimately exceeded Mach two. There is no doubt that the D-558-2 was one of the most beautiful airplanes ever built and flown. McDonnell Douglas

The Lockheed TF-80C (formerly TP-80C), flown first by Lockheed test pilot Tony LeVier, was built to demonstrate the need for a two-seat trainer and transition aircraft for jet-powered fighter pilots. Ultimately, the two-seat TF-80C metamorphosed into the T-33A T-Bird, the mainstay of the USAF Air Training Command until the advent of the T-38A Talon. The third pre-production TF-80C is shown. Lockheed

There wasn't much left of the number two YB-49 after its crash on June 5, 1948, some 12mi northwest of Muroc AAF; its total flight time was fifty-eight hours, two minutes. All crewmen were killed: Maj. Daniel H. Forbes Jr. (pilot), Capt. Glen W. Edwards (copilot), 1st Lt. Edward L. Swindell (bombardier/navigator), and civilians Clare C. Lesser and C. H. LaFountain. AFFTC/HO via Tony Landis

The one-of-a-kind Curtiss XF-87 Blackhawk prototype flies above the Mojave Desert close to Muroc AAF during one of its early test hops. Originally designed as a light attack bomber, designated XA-43, the Blackhawk in- stead became a heavy fighter. Comfort and all-around visibility for its pilots were exceptional, as this view il- lustrates. USAF via AFFTC/HO

The one-of-a-kind Northrop XF-89 Scorpion prototype wings its way over the Tehachapi Mountains during an early flight test out of Muroc AAF. This and its YF-89A stablemate led to full-scale production of one of the US-AF's first limited all-weather night fighters: the F-89 series of Scorpions. USAF via AFFTC/HO

Nicknamed Bumble Bee *and named* Goblin, *the first of two McDonnell XF-85s rests on its transport dolly at Muroc with McDonnell test pilot "Ed" Schoch under glass. By all appearances, its pilot seemed to straddle the 3,000lb-thrust Westinghouse turbojet engine power-* ing the mini-jet. Moreover, its fuselage looked more like an engine nacelle than a fuselage. Both XF-85s have survived. One is in the U.S. Air Force Museum, and the other is at the outdoor museum at Offutt AFB, Nebraska. USAF via AFFTC/HO

The Convair XF-92A Dart has the distinction of being the world's first delta-winged airplane to fly. It appears here in its natural all-metal finish prior to being painted all-white for improved visibility during later flight-test phases. The airplane, albeit underpowered, was exten- sively flown at Muroc by Convair, USAF, and NASA test pilots. Though not a very successful performer, the Dart led to the later delta-winged F-102 and F-106 all- missile-armed, all-weather interceptors. USAF via AFFTC/HO

First of the three USAF Penetration Fighters, the number one XF-88 Voodoo is shown during its first flight at Muroc AAF; McDonnell test pilot "Bob" Edholm is at the stick. The XF-88, in contention with the Lockheed XF-90 and North American YF-93, was judged best. As it worked out, though, none of them were ever ordered into full-scale production. A later version of the XF-88, the F-101 Voodoo, was produced. McDonnell Douglas

The first of two Northrop X-4 Bantams lifts off at Muroc on one of its test hops. This X-4 survives and is on static display at the USAF Academy, Colorado Springs, Colorado. The number two X-4 is at the U.S. Air Force Museum. AFFTC/HO via Tony Landis

The second of two Republic XF-91 Thunderceptors after its radar nose—a la F-86D—had been installed. With the additional thrust provided by its 6,000lb-thrust rocket motor, the single turbojet-powered XF-91 became the first jet-powered airplane to exceed Mach one in level flight, attaining 1,125mph at 50,000ft. Built under Project MX-909, production F-91s were to be all-out interceptor aircraft optimized for the destruction of enemy bomber aircraft in and around U.S. airspace. Note the giant auxiliary drop-type fuel tanks and two-wheel main landing gears. USAF via AFFTC/HO

Right
Edwards Air Force Base, formerly Muroc Air Force Base, is named for Capt. Glen W. Edwards who died on June 5, 1948, in the crash of the number two YB-49 Flying Wing bomber he was copiloting. A native of Lincoln, California, Captain Edwards was born March 5, 1918. In July 1941, shortly after graduation from the University of California, he enlisted as an aviation cadet in the U.S. Army Air Corps. Nine months later, he was commissioned second lieutenant and received his pilot wings. He won four Distinguished Flying Crosses and six Air Medals during World War II for flying fifty bombing missions over Europe in Douglas A-20 Havoc attack bombers. Following WWII, he became an outstanding experimental test pilot and was assigned to Muroc AAF on November 25, 1944. Muroc AFB was renamed Edwards AFB on December 8, 1949. During the official dedication ceremony on January 27, 1950, it was said that Captain Edwards' outstanding devotion to duty would become an inspiration for all who would follow in this and future generations at Edwards AFB. In fact, a number of test pilots simply refer to Edwards as "Eddie's." USAF via AFFTC/HO

With Lockheed test pilot Tony LeVier at its controls, the first of two Lockheed XF-90 Penetration Fighters flies near Muroc AAF. With two afterburning 4,200lb-thrust Westinghouse turbojet engines, the redesignated XF-90A was able to attain 1.12 Mach number in an over-the-top dive from 30,000ft; on the level, it only had a top speed of 668mph at 1,000ft. Lockheed

The first of two North American YF-86D (formerly YF-95A) Sabre "Dog" service-test aircraft flies near Edwards AFB. The two YF-86Ds proved successful and, as a result, this version of the Sabre—armed only with unguided rockets—went into full-scale production. Rockwell via Chris Wamsley

Chapter 2

Mach Busters

The 1950s

**The rocket aircraft were, and are, an important
part of aviation history.**
—Neil Armstrong

By the 1950s, Edwards Air Force Base was one busy aircraft flight-test and evaluation site. What local residents had called "the foreign legion of the Army Air Corps" by the end of the late-1930s, had become a mecca for the U.S. armed forces and government agencies such as the National Advisory Committee on Aeronautics (NACA), the predecessor of the National Aeronautics and Space Administration (NASA). The 1940s had seen Edwards become the home of aviation records, advancements, and achievements—the once elusive sound barrier penetrated and surpassed by both rocket- and turbojet-powered aircraft. As a major base, it had become an important

The first of two Lockheed YF-97A (later YF-94C) Starfire service-test aircraft poses on Muroc Dry Lake in early-January 1950. Powered by a single afterburning Pratt & Whitney J48 turbojet engine (a license-built derivative of the Rolls-Royce Tay), this version of the Starfire featured an all-missile armament, the Hughes E-5 *fire control system, and AN/APG-40 radar set. It was capable of 0.80 Mach number speed in level flight and, in full production dress, it carried forty-eight unguided 2.75in-diameter folding-fin aircraft rockets and was capable of limited all-weather operation. Lockheed*

stepping stone toward the future that ultimately allowed mankind to leave planet Earth, visit the moon, and reach toward the stars. By the end of the 1940s, a manned air vehicle had climbed to 71,902ft (about 13.5mi), while another had sped to 1.45 Mach number (about 950mph).

During the 1950s, however, much greater speeds and heights would be attained by the exclusive breed of dedicated flight-test pilots based at Edwards.

1950

A multitude of new aircraft arrived at Edwards for testing in the 1950s, primarily fighters and research aircraft.

Tony LeVier accomplished a successful flight on the first of two service-test YF-97A (redesignated YF-94C on September 12, 1950) single-jet aircraft on January 19, 1950. This airplane was the forerunner of the USAF's limited all-weather, all-missile-armed F-94C Starfire fighter-interceptor.

Six days later on January 25, North American's George Welch successfully flight tested the first of two service-test YF-93A (formerly YP-86C) aircraft. It had been trucked to Edwards from North American's Inglewood, California, facility and it would be the third and last entry in a trio of Penetration Fighter contestants.

Tragedy struck less than one month later, when two serious crashes saw one person killed and two aircraft lost.

The first of these two tragedies happened on February 22 when the Northrop XF-89 Scorpion prototype crashed after departing Edwards for a flight back to Hawthorne. During a high-speed pass over Northrop Field, aluminum skins on the right horizontal stabilizer began to peel off. Then the whole tail group and a wing ripped off. With no way to control the airplane, a crash followed. Northrop test pilot Charles Tucker was seriously injured, and Northrop flight-test engineer Arthur A. Turton was killed. The airplane was to return to Edwards that day.

The second crash occurred at Edwards on March 15 when, during a high-speed taxi test in which its nose landing gear experienced a severe

The first of two North American YF-93A service-test articles shows the type's original NACA-developed flush-type engine air intake system. The idea was to eliminate unwanted parasite drag, however, the inlets were too *small to provide adequate air to the YF-93A's single afterburning Pratt & Whitney J48 turbojet engine. The inlets were later modified for improved performance.*
Rockwell

shimmy, the last surviving service-test Northrop YB-49 Flying Wing was destroyed. There were no deaths this time, luckily, as all crew members escaped without serious injuries.

On May 4, after lifting off at Hawthorne, the one-of-a-kind service-test Northrop YRB-49A Flying Wing reconnaissance bomber landed at Edwards for ongoing evaluation. This six-jet, like its eight-jet YB-49 sister, was found to be a less-than-spectacular performer, and in mid-1950, the proposed RB-49A program was canceled and the YRB-49A scrapped. Thus, until the Northrop B-2 appeared in 1988, no Flying Wing bomber aircraft existed after October 1953.

A turbopropjet-powered development of the Douglas AD-1 Skyraider, the first of two prototype

Douglas XA2D-1 Skyshark aircraft, arrived by truck at Edwards in early-May 1950 from Douglas' El Segundo, California, facility. It made a successful first flight on May 26, with Douglas test pilot George Jansen at the controls.

Next up was Republic's YF-96A (later redesignated YF-84F) Thunderstreak. Following its cross-country airlift to Edwards from Republic's facility at Farmingdale, New York, Republic test pilot Oscar P. "Bud" Haas flew this sweptback-winged version of the straight-winged F-84 Thunderjet on its maiden flight on June 3.

Twenty-four days later, on June 27, Northrop project pilot John J. Quinn took the Northrop YF-89A Scorpion on its first flight at Edwards. The one-of-a-kind YF-89A was originally to be XF-89

The one-of-a-kind Northrop YRB-49A Flying Wing pho-to-reconnaissance bomber as it appeared during its first flight from Hawthorne to Edwards. As a six-jet air- *plane, it was powered by six non-afterburning Allison J35 turbojets, two in underwing pod-type nacelles and four buried within the wing. USAF via AFFTC/HO*

Had it been produced, the Douglas A2D-1 Skyshark was to be a faster, more fuel-efficient version of its AD-1 (later A-1) Skyraider predecessor. The first of two prototype XA2D-1 airplanes is shown during an early test hop near Edwards AFB. Powered by the troublesome 5,100hp Allison XT40-A-2 propeller-turbine engine (actually two Allison T38s) driving contra-rotating propellers through a common gearbox, the XA2D-1 failed to earn production status. In addition to the pair of XA2D-1s, six of ten pre-production A2D-1s were built and flown. A full-scale production contract, however, was not forthcoming. McDonnell Douglas

number two, but after its extensive modification program, it was redesignated as a service-test example of the Scorpion.

From June 29 to July 7, 1950, the long-awaited Penetration Fighter fly-off competition was held among the McDonnell XF-88A, Lockheed XF-90A, and North American YF-93A. And though the Penetration Fighter program had already been terminated, the investment of U.S. tax dollars and research time demanded that a winner be declared. Ultimately, the USAF decided that McDonnell's entry was the best of this trio. A redesigned version of the winning XF-88A would later emerge as the famed McDonnell F-101 Voodoo.

After its arrival from Lockheed's Van Nuys facility, Tony LeVier made a successful first flight on the Lockheed YF-94B version of the Starfire on September 28. Oddly, due to its higher program priority, the C model of the Starfire had flown before the B model; this rarely occurs.

1951

On January 23, 1951, with Douglas test pilot Robert Rahn at its controls, the first of two proto-

type Douglas XF4D-1 Skyray aircraft made its first successful flight. It was soon joined by XF4D-1 number two, which likewise made its first flight at Edwards.

On February 4, in an effort to better consolidate current flight-test activities, the USAF Test Pilot School moved to Edwards AFB from Wright-Patterson AFB in Dayton, Ohio. This move allowed student test pilots to gain first-hand flight-test experience and knowledge at the USAF's major outpost of such activities.

To achieve the high-g-force maneuvering goals now being pursued at Edwards, base flight-doctors needed to learn how much positive and negative gs a man's body could withstand before he blacked out. The best and safest way to perform these tests was in a controlled environment on the ground. To that end, various high-speed, rail-mounted, rocket-powered sleds were developed. Following a number of ground-based tests in late-1950 and early-1951, the rocket sleds were ready for all-out performance evaluations in mid-1951.

On June 1 at Edwards' North Base area, USAF Maj. John P. Stapp was strapped into a rocket-powered sled aimed down a 2,000ft-long deceleration track. A single 4,000lb-thrust rocket motor instantly launched him down the track and into its braking system; in just 18ft, he came to a full stop from 88.6mph. Maj. Stapp had endured 45gs with about 500gs per second rate of onset. In other words, his body had absorbed a sudden impact of more than 8,000lb.

On June 20, with Bell test pilot Jean "Skip" Ziegler in its seat, the first of two swing-wing X-5 airplanes made its first successful flight at Edwards. Developed under the MX-1095 project, the Bell X-5 featured a swing wing for variable aft sweepback angles, from 20 to 60deg. These early swing-wing tests at Edwards led to the successful development of the General Dynamics F-111 and the Grumman F-14 during the 1960s and 1970s, respectively.

During an official USAF ceremony at Edwards AFB on June 25, the Air Force Flight Test Center (AFFTC) and its motto "Toward the Unexplored" (*Ad Inexplorata* in Latin) was activated.

Bell again took to the air on July 20, when NACA's Joe Cannon made the first glide flight on Bell's X-1 number three. This was followed on July 31 with its first powered flight, flown by NACA's A. Scott Crossfield.

Right
In a successful effort to increase performance in the transonic speed regime, Republic redesigned its Thunderjet series of F-84s to create the swept-winged Thunderstreak—the F-84F. Shown is the service YF-84F (formerly YF-96A) Thunderstreak. Republic via Mike Machat Illustration

Originally powered by an inadequate 5,000lb-thrust Allison J35 turbojet engine, while awaiting availability of an equally inadequate 7,000lb-thrust Westinghouse XJ40 jet engine, the second of two prototype XF4D-1 Skyray aircraft (shown) did prove its airworthiness on a grand scale. In fact, after the initial F4D-1 (later F-6A)

Skyray was outfitted with a 9,700lb-thrust Pratt & Whitney J57 turbojet engine, it exceeded the speed of sound during its maiden flight in level flight and climbed like the proverbial bat out of hell. McDonnell Douglas

On July 24, Jean Ziegler made the first and only flight on the Bell X-1D airplane. Following a successful glide flight on that date, the craft's nose landing gear gave way and the plane was damaged; Ziegler was not hurt. After the second-generation X-1 was repaired, it went up for its first powered flight on August 22. A Boeing EB-50A was the mother ship. Its pilot, USAF Lt. Col. Frank K. Everest Jr. noticed a very low reading on the nitrogen gas pressure gauge, and after talking with onboard Bell engineers, the X-1D's propellants were jettisoned and the mission was aborted. As the propellants were being jettisoned, there was an explosion and fire at the X-1D's aft end. After Frank Everest was safely out of the air vehicle, it was dropped, and it smashed into the desert floor about 2mi southwest of Muroc Dry Lake. Thus, the one-of-a-kind X-1D never did make a powered flight.

On August 7, while piloting D-558-2 number one, Douglas test pilot Bill Bridgeman zoom-climbed to a new altitude record of 74,494ft (14.1mi). When D-558-2 was delivered to NACA's High Speed Flight Station at Edwards just three weeks later, it had been flown 122 times by USN, USMC, and Douglas pilots.

The second of two Bell X-5s made a successful first flight at Edwards on December 10, with Bell's "Skip" Ziegler in control.

Following extensive flight-test activities elsewhere, the second of two Martin XB-51 trijet medium bomber prototype aircraft arrived at Edwards on December 14 for a series of high-speed bombing tests. Three days later, on December 17, 1951, on the forty-seventh anniversary of the Wright Brothers' first flight, XB-51 number two made its first flight from Edwards AFB.

Bell X-5 number one, shown here on its first flight over Rogers Dry Lake, still lives at the U.S. Air Force Museum at Wright-Patterson AFB in Ohio. X-5 number two *was lost during a spin recovery test at Edwards on October 14, 1953, which caused the death of USAF Maj. Raymond Popson. AFFTC/HO via Tony Landis*

1952

On February 18, 1952 USAF Brig. Gen. J. Stanley Holtoner became base commander, serving until May 19, 1957.

The one-of-a-kind Republic YRF-84F, the service-test photographic reconnaissance version of the production RF-84F Thunderflash aircraft, made its successful first flight at Edwards on February 18. It was flown by Republic test pilot Carl A. Bellinger.

On March 21, XB-51 number two experienced an in-flight mishap during which its left rear landing gear door opened. This caused severe buffeting which, in turn, caused the number two tail-mounted engine to fail; however, the airplane was safely landed.

During a high-speed structural demonstration on May 9, 1952, XB-51 number two came apart in the air and crashed. Its pilot, USAF Maj. Neil H. Lathrop, then chief of the flight-test branch at Edwards, was killed; he was the only crewman on board.

After its arrival at Edwards from Grumman's Bethpage, New York, facility in early-May 1952, the one-of-a-kind Grumman XF10F-1 Jaguar was prepared for flight-test activities. Proposed as a swing-wing carrier-based fighter for the U.S. Navy, the XF10F-1 made a successful first flight on May 19 at the hands of Grumman test pilot Corwin H. "Corky" Meyer.

Under USAF project MX-656, which had been delayed because of engine development and airframe construction problems, the one-of-a-kind Douglas X-3 Stiletto finally arrived at Edwards in early-October 1952. On October 20, Douglas test pilot William B. "Bill" Bridgeman made its first flight. He flew the airplane another twenty-four times before it was handed over to the USAF which, after six flights, turned it over to NACA, which flew it twenty times before it was retired. Although it had been designed for double-sonic speeds, and looked like it was flying at triple-sonic speeds while static on the ground, it only achieved

The third of three first-generation Bell X-1 air vehicles rolls to a stop after its one and only flight– an unpowered glide flight on July 20, 1951. Following a captive flight on November 9, 1951, X-1 number three was destroyed during static ground operations while still mated to its B-50 carrier plane. USAF via AFFTC/HO

Originally ordered from Martin as the prototype XA-45 light attack bomber under Project MX-838, then reclassified as a light bombardment airplane, the XA-45 was redesignated XB-51. Two examples were built featuring three 6,000lb-thrust General Electric J47 turbojet engines (one in the tail, one on either side of the forward fuselage), a T-tail, and a proposed bomb load of 10,400lb. Often called the Flying Cigar by those who flew it, the first of two XB-51s is shown on the ramp at Edwards, circa late-1952. Note the sun shade over the cockpit canopy. USAF via AFFTC/HO

The service-test Republic YRF-84F Thunderflash rests at Edwards between flight tests to evaluate the type as a high-speed photographic reconnaissance airplane for the USAF. *It featured an F-84E-style cockpit canopy and wing-root engine air inlets to make room for cameras within its solid nose. USAF via AFFTC/HO*

Grumman's development of the XF10F-1 Jaguar was to meet USN requirements for a high-performance carrier-borne swing-wing fighter that could slowly approach and land on aircraft carriers at sea. Only one of two XF10F-1s *that had been ordered was completed. The disappointing, one-of-a-kind XF10F-1 only made thirty-two flights before it was canceled. Grumman*

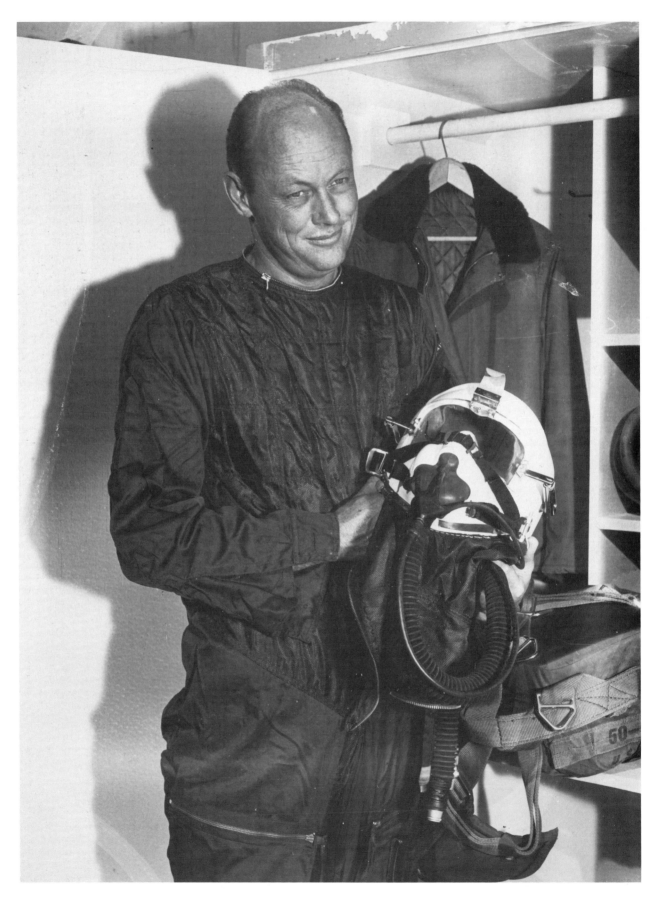

Developed under Project MX-656, Douglas built the X-3 flying Stilleto so that the USAF could gain design experience on possible future high-speed fighters. With a pair of 6,000lb-thrust Westinghouse J46 turbojet engines, it was to fly at 2.0 Mach number at 35,000ft for at least ten minutes. But as the J46 developed, its diameter became too large to fit in the X-3's fuselage, which was already being built. Thus, to get the airplane flying (the program was already behind schedule), a pair of 4,900lb-thrust Westinghouse J34 turbojet engines were substituted. Consequently, with less thrust than what it was designed for, the X-3 barely exceeded the speed of sound during flight test—1.21 Mach number (its maximum speed) was recorded on July 28, 1953, in a dive. Two X-3s were ordered, but only the one shown was built. USAF via AFFTC/HO

a high speed mark of 1.21 Mach number, and it took a 30deg dive from 30,000 to 35,000ft to accomplish that.

The first of two twinjet Douglas XA3D-1 Skywarrior prototypes was trucked to Edwards from Douglas' El Segundo facility and made its successful first flight October 28. Douglas test pilot George Jansen was at the controls.

The first level flight speed in excess of Mach number one was achieved December 9, 1952, by the number two Republic XF-91 Thunderceptor. The Republic fighter's total thrust output of 11,200lb, developed by a turbojet engine and a rocket motor, pushed the XF-91 to 1.07 Mach number. Republic pilot "Rusty" Roth's flight marked the first time that a dedicated combat-type airplane had exceeded the speed of sound in level-attitude flight.

1953

Bell's "Skip" Ziegler made the first glide flight on the second-generation X-1A February 14, 1953; seven days later, he made the first powered flight on this new breed of X-1 air vehicles.

On February 28, the number one Martin XB-51 arrived at Edwards after a ferry flight from Wright-Patterson AFB (it had first flown at Martin's facility October 28, 1949). Like its counterpart that had crashed in 1952, it was scheduled to participate in a series of high-speed bombing tests from March 1, 1953, to March 1, 1954. Maj. Chuck Yeager was project pilot. This particular airplane went on to star as the XF-120 "Gilbert Fighter" in the Warner Brothers movie Toward the Unknown. (The airplane was lost March 25, 1956, during

Left
Douglas test pilot Bill Bridgeman suits up for yet another flight test of the Douglas X-3 Stilleto. Bridgeman, the only Douglas pilot to fly the Stilleto, flew it on twenty-five of its fifty-one flights. One of the more famed test pilots of the 1950s, Bridgeman was killed in 1958 while off duty and riding as a passenger in a Grumman Goose en route to Catalina Island from Long Beach, California. McDonnell Douglas via Harry Gann

filming when it crashed on takeoff from El Paso, Texas. Like the earlier XB-51 number two, pilot error was the cause.)

Flight testing of the one-of-a-kind XF10F-1 Jaguar came to an end following thirty-two successful, albeit unimpressive, test flights at Edwards. Grumman's "Corky" Meyer had performed all testing. Much like Bell's X-5—America's first swing-wing airplane—the XF10F-1 did not fare well. Both designs paved the way for future, successful swing-wing designs, however.

North American's George Welch made a successful first flight on the one-of-a-kind North American YF-86H Sabre on April 30, 1953. This fifth version of the Sabre Jet was optimized as a fighter-bomber and was one of the more successful variants after it was placed into full-scale production.

On May 12, Bell X-2 number two was carried aloft by its EB-50A mother ship for a powered flight. As the mother ship began to pass over California's Lake Ontario on its way to the preplanned launch point, the X-2 exploded while still attached to its shackles. The force of the explosion caused the X-2 to detach from its shackles and fall away from its carrier plane. Although the EB-50A survived the incident, both X-2 pilot Jean Ziegler and an on-board observer, Frank Wolko, were killed. X-2 number two plummeted to the lake's bottom where it remains to this day. It was later deter-

The first of two Douglas XA3D-1 Skywarrior prototypes (shown) wings its way across the Mojave Desert on its first flight in late-1952. Following the flight-test of two XA3D-1s and one YA3D-1, it became apparent that Dou- *glas had produced a winner. Ultimately, 283 A-3 (formerly A3D) Skywarriors were built for the USN. Mc-Donnell Douglas*

mined that the explosion's cause was a faulty Ulmer leather gasket that allowed the X-2's rocket fuel to mix prematurely. The blow-up occurred just as the fuel system was starting to be pressurized with nitrogen gas.

A major event occurred May 25 when the first of two service-test North American YF-100 Super Sabre aircraft made its first flight at Edwards. Piloted by North American's George Welch, the airplane attained a Mach number of 1.10 at 35,000ft while flying straight and level. This was the first time that a turbojet-only-powered combat-type airplane had exceeded Mach one in level flight. To prove it was not a fluke, Welch repeated his flight that very same day. These achievements were verified by Frank Everest, who flew chase in an F-86 Sabre, the YF100's predecessor, on both flights; at 0.90 Mach, the YF-100 passed him like he was sitting still.

On August 21, USMC test pilot Lt. Col. Marion Carl flew the number two Douglas D-558-2 Skyrocket to a new unofficial altitude record of 83,235ft or 15.7mi. This would be the peak altitude reached by any Skyrocket. It should be clarified here that all records (altitude and speed) for the rocket-powered air vehicles were *unofficial* because they were air-launched.

Tragedy struck again October 14. USAF test pilot Maj. Raymond Popson was killed when the number two Bell X-5 crashed after entering a spin from which it did not recover. Proving the old adage "life goes on," George Welch completed a successful first flight on the number two North American YF-100 Super Sabre that same day. The number one North American X-10, built under project MX-770 as a remotely piloted vehicle (RPV) for the proposed SM-64 Navaho project, was also successfully flight tested that day.

Ten days later, on October 24, Convair flight-test pilot Richard L. "Dick" Johnson piloted the first of two delta-winged service-test examples of the Convair YF-102 Delta Dagger. Although the airplane did not achieve supersonic speed as had been planned, its first flight was aerodynamically

The third of three service-test Republic Aviation YF-84F Thunderstreaks (background) flies in formation with its *proposed successor, the Republic XF-91 Thunderceptor.* USAF via AFFTC/HO

The first of three second-generation Bell X-1s, the Bell X-1A returns for a lake bed landing after one of its powered flights. The X-1A's best speed was 2.44 Mach number (1,650mph), and its best altitude was 90,440ft (17.12mi). AFFTC/HO via Tony Landis

The second of three second-generation Bell X-1s, the Bell X-1B glides toward Rogers Dry Lake following a powered flight. The X-1B's best speed was 2.3 Mach number (1541mph); its best altitude was 65,000ft (12.31mi). AFFTC/HO via Tony Landis

The first of two North American YF-86H Sabre Jet service-test airplanes, piloted by North American test pilot George Welch, flies over Edwards on its first flight. The F-86H was a dedicated fighter-bomber derivative of the F-86 line. Rockwell via Chris Wamsley

successful. This was attributed to the earlier flights of the Convair XF-92A Dart program.

Records continued to fall in 1953. On November 20, NACA test pilot A. Scott Crossfield became the first man to pilot an air vehicle to double-sonic speed when, after being air-launched, he flew D-558-2 Skyrocket number two to a speed of 2.005 Mach number (1,291mph) while passing through 62,000ft in a dive from 72,000ft.

Not to be outdone, USAF Maj. Chuck Yeager shattered Crossfield's new mark on December 12 while piloting the one-of-a-kind Bell X-1A over Rogers Dry Lake. Yeager's new mark, 2.44 Mach number (1,640mph), would stand some thirty-five months. It was during this high-speed flight that Yeager first experienced inertia coupling (then known as high-speed instability) when, just after reaching 2.44 Mach number, the second-generation X-1A fell violently out of control. Though his ride was spinning about all three flying axes (pitch, roll, and yaw) simultaneously, Yeager somehow managed to recover to level flight and make a safe deadstick (unpowered) landing on Rogers Dry Lake. Unfortunately, this deadly problem was to plague flight-test activities at Edwards for some time to come.

1954

After its arrival by truck to Edwards in late-1953, YF-102 number two made a successful first flight on January 11, 1954; Convair's Dick Johnson was the pilot. But even with several modifications, it could not exceed Mach number one—not even in a dive. The F-102's success had to wait.

In mid-February 1954, the third so-called Century Series of USAF jet fighters, the Lockheed XF-104 Starfighter, arrived by truck from Lockheed's Burbank facility. During a high-speed taxi run on February 28, the number one prototype XF-104 (two would be tested) made an unofficial first flight when it skipped off Rogers Dry Lake and flew some 5ft off the ground for about 300yd. Its first official flight was on March 5, with Lockheed's Tony LeVier on board.

An improved version of the Republic F-84F Thunderstreak, the YF-84J—unofficially dubbed *Thunderstreak II*—made its first flight at Edwards May 7, 1954, with Republic's "Rusty" Roth at the controls.

On June 16, Lockheed test pilot Herman R. "Herm" Salmon made the first flight on the Lockheed XFV-1 vertical takeoff and landing (VTOL) airplane. This particular VTOL airplane competed with the Convair XFY-1, which made its first and subsequent flights elsewhere. Neither type proved a success nor entered into production.

The one-of-a-kind XA4D-1 Skyhawk prototype was successfully flight tested at Edwards by Douglas test pilot Robert Rahn on June 22. This airplane was the forerunner of the famed A-4 Skyhawk aircraft series. Produced between 1954 and 1979, it had a longer production life than any other combat-type aircraft in the free world. Ultimately, 2,960 A-4s in numerous models were produced.

A USAF derivative of the USN's A3D (later A-3) Skywarrior—the premier Douglas RB-66A Destroyer, the first of five pre-production RB-66As—took off at Douglas' Long Beach facility on June 28. After a successful maiden flight with Douglas test pilot George Jansen in control, made a good landing at Edwards for ongoing flight-test action.

The B-52's ill-fated competition was Convair's YB-60, shown here with a B-36 from which it was derived. USAF via AFFTC/HO

On August 5, USAF Col. Frank Everest made the first glide flight of Bell X-2 number one. (Its first powered flight, again with Colonel Everest on board, would not occur until November 11, 1955, when it was air-launched by its Boeing EB-50D mother ship. Its powered flight had been delayed because of damage suffered during its second landing following its second glide flight on March 8, 1955.)

Lockheed test pilots Stanley Betz (pilot) and Roy Wimmer (copilot) successfully flew the second of two Lockheed YC-130 Hercules service-test aircraft from Lockheed Air Terminal at Burbank, California, to Edwards AFB on August 23. Number two flew first because number one underwent static structural loads testing prior to its first flight.

USAF Maj. "Kit" Murray piloted the Bell X-1A to a new unofficial altitude record of 90,440ft

(17.1mi) on August 26. This altitude permitted Major Murray to reportedly become the first man to actually see the Earth's curvature.

USAF Lt. Col. Jack Ridley made the first unpowered glide flight of the Bell X-1B on September 24. The X-1B's first powered flight, flown by USAF Maj. "Kit" Murray, followed shortly thereafter on October 8.

The first of twenty-nine research, development, test, and evaluation McDonnell F-101A Voodoos was successfully flown on September 29 by McDonnell test pilot Robert C. "Bob" Little. As you may recall, it was McDonnell's earlier success with the XF-88A Penetration Fighter contestant that led to the advent of the USAF's fourth Century Series jet fighter; unlike its XF-88A predecessor, the F-101 went into full-scale production.

A new 15,000ft (2.8mi) runway on the south-

Boeing's XB-52 (foreground) and YB-52 aircraft were fore-runners of the venerable B-52 Stratofortress bomber. After
initial testing at Boeing's Washington state facilities, they were ferried to Edwards for ongoing tests. Boeing

First flown on May 25, 1953, the North American YF-100 Super Sabre was the first USAF jet fighter to exceed the speed of sound in level-attitude flight. Amazingly, it did so on its very first flight, repeating the feat later the same day. Rockwell via Chris Wamsley

ern edge of Rogers Dry Lake was dedicated on October 12 during a high-visibility ceremony. At that time, the new runway was the USAF's longest. That very same day, unfortunately, still another tragic crash slowed the rapid progress being made at Edwards AFB.

North American chief test pilot George Welch was performing a high-speed, high-g structural demonstration on the ninth production F-100A Super Sabre. After departing North American's Palmdale, California, facility, about 30mi south of Edwards AFB, he flew the airplane to an altitude of about 40,000ft over Rogers Dry Lake. He then nosed over and entered into a 30deg dive toward Rosamond Dry Lake within the boundaries of Edwards AFB. When he reached 1.40 Mach number and 7-plus gs, the dreaded inertia coupling phenomenon surfaced. His airplane immediately went out of control, spinning violently about all three axes, and then disintegrated. Unable to regain control or eject from the wildly gyrating airplane,

Welch rode what was left of it into the ground. It was later determined that his airplane, and others that had experienced inertia coupling, did not have enough vertical tail and wing area. After these modifications were made to subsequent F-100s, the problem, for the most part, was cured.

Right
A World War II ace with sixteen kills, George S. "Wheaties" Welch joined North American Aviation after the war to serve as a test pilot. He eventually became chief test pilot, and on October 12, 1954, while testing the ninth production F-100A Super Sabre, he was killed during a test to demonstrate the type's maximum-g at maximum Mach number. In a dive from 45,000ft toward Rosamond Dry Lake, his plane experienced the inertia coupling phenomenon and disintegrated. He ejected but was fatally injured, when the airplane broke apart in the cockpit area, shredding Welch with ripped and torn metal. Rockwell

Since neither service-test Convair YF-102 Delta Daggers were capable of supersonic speed, Convair undertook a rapid modification program on the airframe. Convair applied the Area Rule theory developed by NACA's Richard T. Whitcomb, in which the aircraft's fuselage was pinched-in to form a Coke-bottle shape. After this modification, the new YF-102A made its first flight on December 20, 1954, with Convair's Dick Johnson at the controls. Aerodynamically stable, Dick Johnson took it up again on the following day to attempt supersonic speed. During his climb-out from Rogers Dry Lake, the airplane easily surpassed Mach one. NACA's Area Rule, designed to eliminate drag in the transonic speed regime of 600–800mph, worked to perfection on Convair's YF-102A, as it did on a number of other aircraft.

1955

After being trucked to Edwards from Dallas, Texas, the first of two XF8U-1 prototype Chance Vought XF8U-1 Crusaders was prepped, then piloted by chief test pilot John W. Konrad on its first flight, March 25, 1955. Konrad hit 1.05 Mach number at 35,000ft while flying straight and level, delivering the USN its first supersonic fighter.

In addition to its twenty-nine-plane order for F-101As, the USAF also ordered two service-test examples of a photo-reconnaissance version of the Voodoo, designated YRF-101A. The first example made its maiden flight at Edwards on June 30, with McDonnell's Bob Little at the controls.

In early-July 1955, a new turbopropjet-powered version of the Republic F-84 appeared at Edwards. Designated XF-84H, the first of two exam-

First flown on March 5, 1954, by Lockheed's famed test pilot Tony LeVier, the first of two prototype Lockheed XF-104 Starfighters (shown) quietly waits on the ramp at North Base for another test hop . Precursor of the world's first double-sonic, level flight fighter, the XF-104, with an interim engine, was able to hit 1.79 Mach number. USAF via AFFTC/HO

The premier service-test Convair YF-102 Delta Dagger rests on Rogers Dry Lake following yet another attempt at supersonic flight . Following an extensive redesign, where NASA's Area Rule theory was adopted, the YF-102's follow-on easily exceeded Mach one—in a climb! USAF via AFFTC/HO

Although it wasn't ordered into full-scale production, the service-test Republic YF-84J Thunderstreak 2 was considered by many to be the ultimate F-84 type. However, by the time it was being tested, it had been overtaken by the progress it had helped create. USAF via AFFTC/HO

ples was initially flight tested on July 22 by Republic test pilot Henry G. Beaird Jr.

Then-director of flight-test activities at Edwards AFB, USAF Col. Horace A. Hanes established a new high-altitude absolute world speed record of 822.135mph on August 20 while flying a factory-stock North American F-100C over a 15km course marked on the Mojave Desert near Palmdale. This was a special speed record, as it was the first time that a turbojet-only-powered airplane had established a world speed record at supersonic speed.

In early-October, the USAF's fifth Century Series jet-powered fighter arrived at Edwards for flight-test activities. On October 22, with Republic test pilot "Rusty" Roth at the stick, the first of two service-test Republic YF-105A Thunderchief aircraft was successfully flown. During the flight, Roth attained 1.05 Mach number in level flight at 35,000ft.

Under USAF project MX-693, the first of two Ryan X-13 Vertijet VTOL aircraft arrived from Ryan's San Diego, California, facility at Edwards in late-November 1955. Its first flight was made in conventional mode on December 10 by Ryan test pilot Pete Girard and was hailed a complete success. (The X-13's first full VTOL demonstration flight did not occur until April 11, 1957, when Girard took off vertically, transitioned to horizontal flight, then transitioned back to vertical for landing. This was a first for a jet-powered VTOL airplane.)

NACA test pilot Dr. Joseph A. "Joe" Walker made the first unpowered glide flight of the Bell X-1E program on December 12, 1955. The one-of-a-kind X-1E was actually X-1 number two of the first-generation series of X-1s extensively modified for higher performance. Just three days after its first glide flight, Joe Walker made its first powered flight. The X-1E's best speed, 2.24 Mach number

Designed as a tail sitter for vertical takeoffs and landings, the Lockheed XFV-1 Salmon shows off its interim horizontal takeoff and landing gear A VTOL-capable engine never materialized. Consequently, the XFV-1 was *restricted to conventional takeoffs and landings throughout its flight-test program at Edwards. Lockheed via Robert F. Dorr*

The first prototype Douglas XA4D-1 Skyhawk, nick-named Heinemann's Hot Rod because it was designed by Ed Heinemann and had a high thrust-to-weight ratio, is shown during its maiden flight at Edwards AFB.

Known later as the A-4, Douglas went on to produce Skyhawks for some twenty-six years (1954–1979) before its manufacture was discontinued. USAF via AFFTC/HO

Derived from the USN's A-3 Skywarrior, the USAF's B-66 Destroyer was created to supersede the obsolete World War II-era Douglas B-26 Invader. Developed as a light tactical bomber and reconnaissance aircraft, the twin-jet

B-66 was also capable of delivering a nuclear punch if required. The number one Destroyer, designated RB-66A (not shown), was very similar to this RB-66B. USAF via AFFTC/HO

Following its first take off at Burbank, and after a successful first flight, the service-test Lockheed YC-130 Hercules—forerunner of the famed C-130 line—made its first landing at Edwards AFB where it underwent flight tests and evaluations. Lockheed

(1,478mph), would be achieved October 8, 1957, during its seventeenth flight. Its best altitude, 73,000-plus feet (about 13.8mi), would occur during its fifteenth flight; Joe Walker piloted both of these flights.

1956

On February 17, 1956, Lockheed test pilot Tony LeVier made the first flight of Lockheed YF-104A number one at Edwards. One day earlier at Lockheed's Burbank facility, the YF-104A Starfighter—which was developed in secrecy—had been rolled-out for the first time publicly. In other words, the public did not know that two XF-104s had already been flying. As it happened, it was the newer and faster YF-104A version that it first learned about.

The first of four pre-production F5D-1 Skylancers, an advanced version of the Douglas F4D-1 (later F-6A) Skyray, was first flown at Edwards on April 21 by Douglas test pilot Robert O. Rahn. Because the type had been bested by Chance Vought's F8U-1 (later F-8A) Crusader, no production orders were forthcoming and all four examples were later leased to NACA for a series of tests, including simulated landings for the upcoming

Reaching a best speed of Mach three-plus and a best altitude of 126,000ft (125,907ft actual), Bell's X-2 was one of the major teachers in the Edwards classroom of high- *speed and high-altitude flight. An X-2 is shown here in the belly of its mother ship prior to a launch. NASA via Tony Landis*

Boeing X-20 Dyna-Soar program (which, ultimately, failed to materialize).

Two days later, on April 23, the number one Douglas C-133A Cargomaster airlifter, piloted by Douglas' J. C. Armstrong, made its first flight from Douglas' Long Beach facility, then landed at Edwards.

One month later on May 23, the one-of-a-kind Douglas X-3 Stilleto made its last flight at Edwards. It was piloted by NACA test pilot Joe Walker. All in all, the X-3 had only flown fifty-one times since its arrival at Edwards in late-1952; it was soon retired to the U.S. Air Force Museum at Dayton, Ohio, where it is displayed to this day.

Three days later, on May 26, Republic test pilot "Rusty" Roth made a successful first flight on YF-105B Thunderchief number one. This version of the Thunderchief, unlike its YF-105A counterpart, was capable of double-sonic speeds in level flight, whereas the former could only attain super-

sonic speeds on the level. NACA's Area Rule and a more powerful engine made the difference.

One very impressive unofficial world altitude mark was set on September 7 when USAF Capt. Iven C. Kincheloe piloted the number one Bell X-2 to a maximum altitude of 125,907ft (23.8mi). Although he had flown above 99 percent of the Earth's atmosphere, newspaper reporters were incorrect when they dubbed Captain Kincheloe "the first of the spacemen."

In late-August 1956, the YF-105B's competition, North American's F-107A Ultra Sabre, arrived at Edwards by truck from North American's Inglewood facility. Originally the B version of the F-100 Super Sabre, the first of three F-107As made its inaugural flight on September 10, with North American test pilot J. Robert "Bob" Baker in its seat.

On September 27, USAF test pilot Capt. Milburn G. "Mel" Apt became the first man to exceed

Derived from its XF-88 Penetration Fighter program of the late-1940s, the premier McDonnell F-101A Voodoo poses on Rogers Dry Lake in late-1954. Second in the so-called USAF Century Series of jet fighters, the F-101 fighter-bomber was to be later adapted to serve as both a fighter-interceptor and a photographic reconnaissance aircraft. USAF via AFFTC/HO

The YF-102A number one was redesigned using NASA's Area Rule and other refinements and turned out to be everything its YF-102 stablemate wasn't. Ultimately, the F-102 metamorphosed into the F-106 which, as it turned out, became the best all-weather, all-missile-armed interceptor ever built. USAF via AFFTC/HO

This aerial view of NASA's Ames-Dryden Flight Research Facility (upper right) at Edwards AFB shows its proximity to Rogers Dry Lake (right), Main Base (center), South Base (lower center), and other parts of Edwards. The circular pattern on the lake bed just to the right (east) of Ames-Dryden is a Compass Rose and is marked with accurate headings for aircraft compass calibrations. Also on the lake bed are markings for runways that have been used for space shuttle landings and for many, many other aircraft's takeoffs and landings. The base housing area is at the upper left. NASA

three times the speed of sound when he piloted the number one Bell X-2 to a top speed of 3.196 Mach number (2,094mph) at 70,000ft. Tragically, due again to inertia coupling, Captain Apt's craft subsequently tumbled violently out of control while he was still flying at more than 2,000mph—he died in the ensuing crash. His unofficial speed record stood for fifty-six months until it was surpassed by an X-15 rocket plane.

The first of two F-106As, originally the B version of the F-102, made its first flight at Edwards on December 26, 1956 with Convair test pilot Dick

Johnson in control. During that first flight, Johnson hit a top speed of 1.90 Mach number at 57,000ft to let everyone know that the Delta Dart—what many have called the best interceptor ever—had arrived.

1957

North American test pilot J. O. Roberts had made the first flight of F-107A number two on November 28, 1956. The third and last example of the short-lived Ultra Sabre was flown on February 18, 1957, by North American test pilot Alvin S. "Al"

The first of two prototype Chance Vought XF8U-1 Crusader airplanes, first flown on March 25, 1955, was the USN's first level-flight supersonic fighter. Powered by an afterburning Pratt & Whitney J57 turbojet engine, it *exceeded Mach one on its first flight to match the US-AF's YF-100 effort some two years earlier. USAF via Arthur L. Schoeni*

White. Having lost out to Republic's F-105 Thunderchief, two of the three F-107As were leased to NACA for its ongoing flight-test activities—designed, as always, to advance aeronautics on the whole—while the number one F-107A was retired to the U.S. Air Force Museum. Even though the Republic F-105 had eliminated the North American F-107, North American officials claimed that the F-107 was the best airplane it had produced to be axed as a final outcome. As it turned out, the F-107 was the last new fighter North American was to develop and fly.

On July 8, 1957, USAF Brig. Gen. Marcus F. Cooper became base commander, a position he would hold until February 6, 1959.

1958

While piloting the number two Grumman F11F-1F Super Tiger above Rogers Dry Lake on April 16, 1958, USN Lt. Cdr. George Watkins set an absolute world altitude record of 76,831ft following a zoom-climb after a maximum performance takeoff at Edwards. At the time, the Grum-

man F11F-1F Super Tiger was in an all-out competition with the Lockheed F-104 Starfighter to see which was preferred by friendly foreign air forces. When the dust finally settled, the Starfighter had prevailed.

Boeing's commercial 707 jetliner, which has spawned the 727, 737, 747, 757, 767, and the new 777 jetliners, made its first flight at Boeing's Renton, Washington, facility on July 15, 1954. This caught all other U.S. airliner manufacturers completely off guard. In time, however, they began to catch up. On May 30, 1958, the first Douglas DC-8 jetliner made its first flight from Douglas' Long Beach facility, and after a two-hour seven-minute flight in the hands of pilot A. G. Heimerdinger, it was safely landed at Edwards AFB for ongoing flight-test action. With the advent of the DC-8, Boeing no longer had a stranglehold on the U.S. jetliner market.

The ultimate version of the Chance Vought Crusader—the XF8U-3 Crusader III, also called the Super Crusader—made its successful first flight at Edwards on June 2, with Chance Vought

Temporarily designated XF-106 because the F-106A was at first to be the F-102B, the first of two Republic XF-84Hs is shown on its first flight at Edwards in mid-1955. As proposed, the Thunderscreech, as it was nick- *named, was to be a long-endurance (fuel-efficient) version of the F-84 series powered by a more economical turbopropjet engine. It also served as a testbed for development of supersonic propellers. USAF via AFFTC/HO*

test pilot John Konrad in its seat. Though optimized for 2.3 Mach number speed, the Crusader III's best speed was not realized until very late in its flight-test program—2.39 Mach number—and after it had lost out to McDonnell's XF4H-1 Phantom II in a fly-off competition.

During a ceremony held in Washington, D.C., on October 1, 1958 the National Advisory Committee on Aeronautics (NACA) became the National Aeronautics and Space Administration (NASA). Therefore, the NACA High Speed Flight Station at Edwards AFB was renamed the NASA Flight Research Facility.

1959

A changing of the guard occurred March 3, 1959, when USAF Maj. Gen. John W. Carpenter III became base commander. He would serve until June 12, 1961.

Under USAF project MX-1226, the first of three North American X-15As made its first captive flight under the right wing of its Boeing B-52A mother ship on March 10, 1959. This was the beginning of one of the most successful Edwards AFB flight-test programs, one in which 4.0, 5.0, and 6.0 Mach numbers would be reached by a manned air vehicle and in which pilots would earn

The second of two Republic service-test YF-105A Thunderchiefs flies above Edwards in early-1956 with its inflight refueling probe extended. Although the J57-powered YF-105A was only capable of Mach one-plus speeds, its follow-on, the J75-powered YF-105B, easily exceeded Mach two. Furthermore, unlike the YF-105A, the YF-105B incorporated NASA's Area Rule. USAF via AFFTC/HO

astronaut wings for flying the X-15A air vehicles to altitudes beyond 300,000ft (50mi-plus).

To answer the USAF's need for a new supersonic trainer in which to train pilots to handle its new class of jet fighters—the F-100, F-101, F-102, F-104, F-105, and F-106—Northrop came up with its service-test YT-38 Talon. On April 10, 1959, with Northrop test pilot Lewis A. "Lew" Nelson under glass, it made a successful forty-minute first flight at Edwards. The type proved viable and, ultimately, replaced Lockheed's highly respected T-33 T-Bird.

The space age was launched on June 8 when the number one X-15A, with North American test pilot A. Scott Crossfield (formerly a NASA test pi-

Right
The USAF's Ryan-built X-13 Vertijet was a complete success. Time and time again, it demonstrated its ability to take off and land vertically on the power of its single non-afterburning Rolls-Royce Avon axial-flow turbojet engine of 10,000lb-thrust. The second of two X-13s is shown hovering by its launch and recovery apparatus. Teledyne Ryan Aeronautical

The last Bell X-1 air vehicle, the X-1E, formerly X-1 number two, flew higher than 73,000ft and faster than 2.2 Mach number during its twenty-six-flight, December 1955 to November 1958 test program. Only two NASA pilots, Joe Walker (twenty-one times) and John McKay (five times), flew the X-1E. NASA

lot) in control, completed its first unpowered glide flight. Its first powered flight—again, with Crossfield as pilot—was September 17.

Northrop's self-financed N-156F Freedom Fighter made its maiden flight June 30 with Lew Nelson at the controls. Northrop gambled its own resources in the hope of winning USAF and friendly foreign air force orders for a supersonic lightweight fighter. (Northrop succeeded in this risky venture in spades. Ultimately, more than 2,600 F-5A/B and F-5E/F aircraft were built.)

Nineteen fifty-nine ended with a brand new absolute world speed record of 2.3 Mach number (1,525.95mph) at 40,550ft by a turbojet-only-powered airplane. USAF Maj. Joseph W. "Joe" Rogers

accomplished this impressive feat in a factory-stock Convair F-106A Delta Dart.

While the 1940s had been a decade of aeronautical teaching, the 1950s were a decade of aeronautical learning. Indeed, the 1950s at Edwards AFB were both productive and lively with considerable growth throughout the bases vast boundaries.

The 1950s saw both double- and triple-sonic speeds surpassed by manned air vehicles, as well as a new all-time altitude mark of 125,000-plus feet attained.

Moreover, many new and advanced types of military aircraft and dedicated research aircraft had been tested. The former led to full-scale production programs for one commercial jetliner, one

After being refined in design and re-engined with a single afterburning General Electric J79 turbojet engine, the service-test YF-104A (first one shown) Starfighter was capable of 2.3 Mach number in level flight. Dubbed the "missile with a man in it" for obvious reasons, the F-104 was yet another classic design from Lockheed's Kelly Johnson. AFFTC/HO via Mary Isham

trainer plane, two cargo aircraft, one attack bomber, one bomber, and fourteen fighter-type airplanes. These aircraft were:
• Douglas DC-8
• Northrop T-38 Talon
• Lockheed C-130 Hercules
• Douglas C-133 Cargomaster
• Douglas A-3 (formerly A3D) Skywarrior
• Douglas B-66 Destroyer
• Republic F-84F and RF-84F Thunderstreak and Thunderflash
• North American F-86H Sabre Jet
• Northrop F-89 Scorpion
• Lockheed F-94B and F-94C Starfire series
• North American F-100 Super Sabre

• McDonnell F-101 and RF-101 Voodoo series
• Convair F-102 and TF-102 Delta Dagger series
• Lockheed F-104 Starfighter
• Republic F-105 Thunderchief
• Convair F-106A and F-106B Delta Dart series
• Northrop F-5 (formerly N-156F) Freedom Fighter
• Douglas F-6 (formerly F4D) Skyray
• Chance Vought F-8 (formerly F8U) Crusader
• Douglas A-4 (formerly A4D) Skyhawk

The 1950s proved to be better than the 1940s, especially in the areas of increased pilot safety and the advancement of aeronautics on the whole. The 1960s, however, would be full of many new surprises.

A Douglas F5D-1 Skylancer, the proposed follow-on to the Douglas F-6 (formerly F4D) Skyray, shuts down on the ramp at NASA's Ames-Dryden Flight Research Facility. Two F5D-1s, experimental USN fighters that were not put into production, were flown by NASA for aeronautical research. NASA flew its F5D-1s until 1970 when they were retired from flight status. NASA

Right
First flown at Convair's Fort Worth, Texas, facility in late-1956, the B-58 Hustler led to the development and USAF's operation of the world's first Mach two bomber airplane. The B-58 underwent extensive tests at Edwards before the type became operational. General Dynamics

Sporting NASA's Area Rule and a higher thrust Pratt & Whitney J75 turbojet engine, the first service-test YF-105B Thunderchief was twice as fast as its earlier YF- *105A counterpart—that is, 2.3 versus 1.3 Mach number. The first YF-105B is shown. AFFTC/HO via Mike Machat Illustration*

Right
The first of two Convair F-106A (formerly F-102B) Delta Dart airplanes banks toward the Main Base complex at Edwards, circa 1957, with its speed brakes deployed. The F-102 was called the Interim Interceptor, and the F-106 was called the Ultimate Interceptor. And, as it turned out, it really was. USAF via AFFTC/HO

Dubbed Ultra Sabre, *the first of three North American F-107As flies above Edwards in late-1956. Featuring a unique dorsal engine air inlet system, specifically designed to best provide air to its single Pratt & Whitney J75 engine, the F-107A competed against—and lost to—Republic's YF-105B in a fly-off competition in mid-1957. Note the F-107A's ventral-mount, semi-recessed nuclear device configuration.* Rockwell via Chris Wamsley

With its cockpit canopy slid aftward to the open position, the first of two Grumman F11F-1F Super Tigers races across Rogers Dry Lake on a medium-speed taxi test prior to its first flight at Edwards on May 25, 1956. This version of Grumman's F-11 (formerly F11F) Tiger, though capable of Mach two-plus speed and zoom-climbs to more than 80,000ft, was not ordered into production. Grumman

With 556 examples built, the Douglas four-jet DC-8 jet-liner proved to be the Boeing 707's most formidable foe. Captained by A. G. Heimerdinger, the first production DC-8 (there was no prototype) is shown during its first flight from Long Beach to Edwards, where its initial flight trials were held. McDonnell Douglas via Mike Machat Illustration

Officially named Crusader III, unofficially called Super Crusader, the Chance Vought XF8U-3 was an all-missile-armed version of the Crusader I and Crusader II series of USN gun- and missile-armed fighter aircraft.

The first of two XF8U-3s is shown during one of its many test hops at Edwards AFB in 1958. Ling-Temco-Vought

*A, Scott Crossfield poses by X-15A number one, circa
1958.* Rockwell via Chris Wamsley

Following its arrival at Edwards, the first of three North American X-15s (shown) was mated to the right wing inboard area of its B-52 mother ship for captive flight-test activities. A second B-52 mother ship is shown in the background. Rockwell via Chris Wamsley

The supersonic Northrop T-38 Talon excelled as a replacement for the subsonic Lockheed T-33 T-Bird. The
first T-38 is shown on a flight test over Edwards in late-
1958. The T-38 was optimized to have a high landing
speed like the Century-series fighters USAF pilots were
being trained to fly. Northrop

The T-38's follow-on, forerunner of the famed F-5 series, was the Northrop model N-156F (later YF-5A) Freedom *Fighter. The first of three Freedom Fighter service-test examples is shown.* Northrop

One of the three Douglas D-558-2 Skyrocket research aircraft flown at Edwards from 1948 to 1956 drops from the belly of a Boeing B-50 launch aircraft during one of its many supersonic research missions. Peak speed was 1,291mph, and peak altitude was 83,235ft. NASA

Among the members of the famed X-series of research air vehicles flown at Edwards during the 1950s are, clockwise from lower left: the Bell X-1A, which studied high speed and high-altitude flight; Douglas D-558-1, which investigated transonic speeds and controllability; Convair XF-92A, first U.S. delta-winged aircraft; Bell X-5, first U.S. variable-sweep-winged aircraft; Douglas D-558-2, first double-sonic airplane; Northrop X-4, which investigated the semi-tailless flying-wing concept; and, center, the Douglas X-3, which investigated sustained supersonic flight. NASA

Chapter 3

Higher Speeds and Higher Altitudes

The 1960s

You can't hoot with the owls all night and expect to soar with the eagles the next day. It just doesn't work that way.

—Chuck Yeager

The many events at Edwards during the 1950s were exhilarating in the truest sense of the word—difficult to surpass most thought. They were wrong. During the 1960s, four, five, and six times the speed of sound would be exceeded by a manned air vehicle: the amazing X-15 rocket plane. Moreover, that same air vehicle flew a number of men beyond the 50mi barrier—high enough to earn them astronaut wings. It was truly a decade filled with higher speeds and higher altitudes.

1960

Following X-15A number one's first unpowered glide flight in mid-1959, it was placed in storage to await the arrival and installation of its planned 57,000lb-thrust rocket motor. X-15A number one was called upon to fly earlier than expected, however, when an engine fire forced an emergency landing of X-15A number two on November 5, 1959. The hard landing caused structural failure of the fuselage as well. A pair of interim 8000lb-thrust rocket motors—16,000lb total thrust, or 41,000lb less than optimum performance required—were fitted to X-15A number one, and on January 23, 1960, it made its first powered flight. With North American test pilot Scott Crossfield at the controls, the two interim motors allowed the number one X-15 to hit 2.53 Mach number (1,669mph) at 66,844ft. Meanwhile, X-15A number two was repaired and, after being equipped with two interim rocket motors like those on X-15A number one, it too joined a series of manufacturer and government flight tests until mid-1960, when it was grounded for installation of its higher thrust and long-awaited rocket motor.

Finally, on November 15, 1960, with Crossfield in control, the design motor made its first flight on X-15A number two; 2.97 Mach number (1,960mph) at 81,200ft was accomplished. The X-15 had arrived.

1961

Aviation history was again made on March 7, 1961, when USAF Maj. Robert M. "Bob" White flew the number two X-15A on the first manned flight beyond four times the speed of sound. On that day, with a single 57,000lb-thrust rocket motor, Major White hit 4.43 Mach number (2,905mph) at an altitude of 77,450ft. White, the new "fastest man alive," was not yet through, however.

On June 23, again piloting X-15A number two, Bob White shot to 5.27 Mach number (3,603mph) at 107,700ft to become the first man to exceed five times the speed of sound.

Much slower and closer to *terra firma*, USAF Maj. Gen. Irving L. Branch became base commander on June 29. Branch held this post until his death January 3, 1966, when the aircraft he was landing at Boeing Field crashed into Puget Sound just northwest of Seattle, Washington.

Another record fell to Maj. Bob White on October 11, again while flying the number two X-15A. On this occasion, Major White flew to a height of 217,000ft (41.09mi) to become the first man to exceed 200,000ft. Although he had *only* flown above 99 percent of Earth's atmosphere, the media immediately hailed him as America's first spaceman.

White liked X-15A number two because every time he flew it, it seemed, he rewrote the record books. He did it again on November 9, 1961, when

Right
NASA test pilot Joseph A. "Joe" Walker, among many other flight-test jobs, flew the North American X-15 twenty-five times. Unfortunately, on June 8, 1966, while flying in a formation flight with the number two XB-70A Valkyrie, his NASA F-104N collided with the Valkyrie's right wing tip and both aircraft went down. Walker and the XB-70A copilot (USAF Maj. Carl S. Cross) were both killed. The cause of the collision remains unclear to this day. NASA

he became the first man to exceed six times the speed of sound, hitting 6.04 Mach number (4,093 mph) at 101,600ft.

1962

Major White's record-setting ways continued in 1962. On July 17, he piloted the number three X-15A, decimating the unofficial world altitude record with his rise to 314,750ft (59.6mi), thus becoming the first man to truly fly an airplane in space (well above 50mi). For this accomplishment, he became the first of eight X-15 test pilots at Edwards to earn their astronaut wings.

On September 18, 1962, while piloting a General Dynamics B-58A Hustler, USAF Maj. Fitzhugh L. "Fitz" Fulton Jr. flew to a record height of 85,360ft (16.16mi) while lifting 11,023lb of payload, thereby breaking a pair of previously Soviet-held records. This record still stands.

1963

On April 18, 1963, with Northrop test pilot Jack Wells in control, the first of two Northrop X-21A airplanes made its first flight out of Northrop's Hawthorne facility, and landed at Edwards AFB. This airplane was designed to investigate full-scale boundary layer control methods for jetliner-size aircraft; both examples were modified Douglas B-66 Destroyer bombers. On August 15, the second Northrop X-21A landed at Edwards after making its first flight out of Hawthorne; again, Jack Wells was the pilot.

The YF-4C (formerly YF-110A), the USAF version of the USN's Phantom II, arrived at Edwards AFB from McDonnell's St. Louis facility in early-May 1963. On May 27, with McDonnell test pilot Bob Little at its controls, the YF-4C was flown successfully.

NASA was working on an air vehicle that uti-

The number one X-15 rocket-powered research airplane leaves its B-52 mother ship for one of its assaults on high-speed and high-altitude. On August 10, 1961, after it received its optimized XLR99 motor, the number one

X-15 hit 4.11 Mach number at 78,200ft. Formerly, its best speed had been 3.50 Mach number with the interim XLR11 motor. NASA

lized the entire structure of the vehicle to produce lift. On August 10, NASA's Milton O. "Milt" Thompson flight tested the NASA M2-F1, the first of NASA's lifting body airplanes. It was the beginning for a new type of aerospace vehicle that ultimately led to America's Space Transportation System and its fleet of space shuttles.

On August 22, with NASA's Joe Walker at the helm, the number three X-15A was piloted to its peak altitude, 354,200ft or 67.08mi. This unofficial world record still stands and, most likely, will never be surpassed.

After a series of contractor test flights, the first of three Lockheed NF-104As was delivered to the Air Force Flight Test Center on October 1. This special version of the famed Starfighter was created to train potential astronauts on the skills of piloting an air vehicle in a weightless environment.

Using a single tail-mounted 6,000lb-thrust rocket motor, in addition to a single turbojet engine, the trio of NF-104As were optimized to zoom-climb to some 125,000ft before returning to base. The second and third NF-104As arrived shortly thereafter.

It took little time for the NF-104A to demonstrate its ability. On November 15, piloted by USAF Maj. Robert W. Smith, an NF-104A zoom-climbed to 118,860ft (22.5mi) above Edwards. That altitude mark lasted only until December 6, when Major Smith zoom-climbed to 120,800ft (22.8mi).

On December 10, 1963, with USAF Aerospace Research Pilot School (now USAF Test Pilot School) commandant Col. Chuck Yeager in control, the number two NF-104A was destroyed in a crash near Mojave. Yeager ejected and, though

continued on page 114

The number two X-15 hangs from the right-hand under-wing pylon mount of NASA B-52A "double-zero-three" as it taxis out to the Edwards runway for one of the 199 research flights in the X-15 program. This B-52A, on loan to NASA from the USAF, was the launch airplane on ninety-three of the 199 research flights. "Double-zero-three" was retired in 1969 and is now located at the Pima County Air Museum, Tucson, Arizona. NASA

Fitzhugh L. "Fitz" Fulton Jr., Lieutenant Colonel USAF (Retired)

Fitz Fulton, now a flight-test consultant living in California, retired from the USAF in 1966 after serving twenty-three years. He retired again in 1986 as chief test pilot for the NASA Ames/Dryden Flight Research Facility after serving twenty years. He then became flight operations director and chief research pilot for Burt Rutan's Scaled Composites Company, where he remained for three years. Fulton has flown over 235 different types of aircraft and has flown some 16,500 hours testing most of the USAF bombers and transports developed since 1950. He flew fifty-five combat missions during the Korean War in the Douglas B-26 Invader, and he's been awarded four Distinguished Flying Crosses, the Harmon Trophy, and many other awards. He was the pilot of the NASA 747 during the five launches of the space shuttle *Enterprise* from its back for that series of unpowered glide tests. The following is a letter written to the author on April 13, 1993.

"I was fortunate to spend many years at Edwards AFB and to fly most of the big supersonic airplanes tested there. Each one was unique. And each one made a significant contribution to the aerospace community and taught us things that only *that* airplane could teach us.

"The Convair B-58 is really my favorite because I was there at the beginning of its test program. I was the project pilot on the first USAF test program and on eight other separate USAF test programs. I feel that I had a part in making it a safer and more capable airplane. I also feel that I knew that airplane as well or better than any other airplane I've ever flown. I flew it above Mach 2 and higher than 85,000ft. The B-58 taught us a great deal about sustained supersonic flight. The fighters at that time could only fly supersonic eight to ten minutes before they had to run for fuel. The B-58 could easily stay supersonic for thirty minutes or more. It could even stay supersonic forty-five to fifty minutes if you [the pilot] were satisfied with speeds of Mach 1.5 or less. The B-58 had some growing pains and it was a very sophisticated airplane that wasn't very forgiving for the pilot who failed to respect it. However, it had excellent handling qualities and a first-rate bombing and navigation system by the time it went into operational service. Strategic Air Command crews won the bombing competition the first time they entered it. The main deficiency, from an operational standpoint, was that it did not have the capability to carry conventional 'iron bombs.' It could only carry nuclear weapons, and that limited its operational usage. Unfortunately, politics played a bigger part in the B-58's acceptability as a first-class weapons system than it deserved.

"The XB-70 was, and still is, our only 'big' airplane that could fly at 3.0 Mach number. I feel that its design and manufacture were quite the accomplishment. Normally it is best to avoid flying a new airplane with a new engine. However, in this case, they were a good match. North American Aviation and General Electric did a good job. Many people ask me why the airplane did not go into production. They don't realize that all plans for its production were dropped several years before its first flight. Its stainless-steel honeycomb sandwich panel construction, high-altitude and high-speed cruise, high cost, and the development of better Soviet radar systems left too many things in question to proceed with its manufacture as a premier weapons system. It was then decided to fund it [two examples] as a pure research project only. We flew them on many missions [Fulton was pilot thirty-one times; copilot thirty-two times] to obtain data for stability and control, handling qualities, supersonic performance, sonic boom characteristics, and inlet and engine performance, as well as on the problems associated with its stainless-steel honeycomb sandwich panel construction. Flying the XB-70 was a relatively high work load for the pilots and the engineers in the control room, who supported us in an outstanding manner. The pilot stayed busy flying the airplane. There was no autopilot. The handling qualities of the XB-70 were certainly acceptable but were a long way from being optimum. The air inlet system for its six engines required almost full-time monitoring by the copilot. All of this had to be done while navigating and doing tests that required changing altitude and speed. The FAA people gave us a certain amount of airspace priority, and once we got above 50,000ft, there wasn't much traffic. Only an occasional U-2 or SR-71. The project was well worth the money spent. The data obtained on the XB-70 program is *still* being used in the planning for the national aerospace airplane.

"The Blackbird program was already mature by the time I got into it in 1970. The USAF was operating the SR-71 version of it to get reconnaissance information in several worldwide locations. The National Aeronautics and Space Administration felt that the airplane could be used to gather and better understand supersonic data. The USAF agreed and assigned NASA two airplanes. The first was a YF-12A, which was left over from the canceled Improved Manned Interceptor program. The second was actually an SR-71A, which had the special cameras and certain electronic equipment removed. It was then redesignated YF-12C. Lockheed had done an outstanding job on the Blackbird series, but sometimes when design problems came out, they had to work hard to find fixes. In doing so, because of other obligations, they didn't always spend the money or the time to learn why their fixes worked. If the fixes worked and did not compromise mission capability, they went on to other problems. NASA looked back at some of these problem areas to get a better technical understanding of why Lockheed's fixes worked. NASA, in conjunction with Lockheed, also developed a better autopilot, found a way of operating the air inlets more efficiently, developed a way of controlling the engine exhaust temperature better, and tested some other airplane and engine improvements. Some of these things were eventually incorporated into the operational fleet of SR-71s and helped to improve their mission capability. NASA used its two Blackbird aircraft to study the problems of high-speed flight and performed several pure research programs with them. One of these, the 'Cold Wall' experiment, was used to calibrate a wind-tunnel for high-speed heat transfer. There was no other way to get an accurate calibration. On those tests, a steel cylinder was fitted to the bottom of one of the airplanes. It was 10ft long and encased with a ceramic shell which was super cooled on the ground and then taken to Mach 3 where the ceramic shell was ballistically removed to expose the cylinder to about 600deg Fahrenheit. The

Blackbird had relatively good handling qualities which were optimized to fly a special mission profile. It was an airplane that was designed to fly above Mach 3 and higher than 80,000ft. It had a good autopilot which relieved the pilot enough that he could do his other duties. The heart of the aircraft's capability to fly fast was the engine air inlet system. That was also automatic. When manual inlet operation was required because of a malfunction, pilot work load became very high.

"Like the B-58 Silverbird, and the XB-70 Whitebird, the Blackbird was a thrill to fly."

Fulton with XB-70A number one.

The famed rocket-powered X-15, flown at NASA's Dryden Flight Research Facility from 1959 to 1968, is one of the most successful research programs ever flown. A wide range of X-15 experiments helped advance the de- *velopment of vital aeronautical and astronautical flight systems. The number three X-15 is shown on Rogers Dry Lake after one of its flights. NASA*

continued from page 111
burned, landed safely after his parachute descent. The primary cause of the accident was non-recovery from a spin that resulted from too much angle of attack (pitchup) and lack of aircraft response. It was later determined that the excessive pitchup was not due to pilot input but a gyroscopic condition set up by the J79 turbojet engine spooling after its shutdown for the rocket-powered zoom-climb phase. The trio of Lockheed NF-104As made 126 successful flights before they were retired from active flight status.

1964

McDonnell's Bob Little made a successful first flight on the YRF-4C (formerly YRF-110A) Phantom II at Edwards on May 18, 1964. This was the photographic reconnaissance version of the F-4C.

To explore the use of lift-fans for vertical take-offs and landings, Ryan was contracted to build two XV-5A air vehicles. After it had been trucked to Edwards from Ryan's San Diego facility, the number one XV-5A made its first flight on May 25. It was flown by Ryan test pilot Lou Everett.

The first of two North American XB-70A Valkyries landed at Edwards for ongoing tests on September 21. It was flown from North American's Palmdale facility by Alvin S. "Al" White, North American chief test pilot, and USAF Col. Joseph F. "Joe" Cotton, USAF project pilot on the B-70 program. The B-70 was originally designed to replace the Boeing B-52 and was to be capable of triple-sonic speeds above 70,000ft. Although it attained those goals, no production B-70s were ever built. Long before the first XB-70A flew, the B-70 program had been canceled, and the two XB-70As were used as high-speed, high-altitude research air vehicles in support of other programs, such as America's Supersonic Transport (SST) project which, as it turned out, never materialized.

1965

The first DC-9 twinjet jetliner, piloted by Douglas' George Jansen, made its premier flight from Long Beach to Edwards on February 25, 1965.

No less than nine absolute world speed and altitude records were established on May 1, 1965. On that day, the Lockheed YF-12A, piloted by USAF Col. Robert L. Stephens and USAF Maj. Walter F. Daniel, set nine records that included a sustained speed of 2,070.102mph (3-plus Mach number) and a sustained altitude of 80,258ft (15.2mi). The YF-12A was a service-test example of the proposed F-12B air defense interceptor that was never produced; also, in a sense, it was the predecessor of the SR-71.

On May 2, after a successful ferry flight from its Fort Worth, Texas, facility, the second of eighteen full-scale development (FSD) General Dynamics F-111A aircraft arrived at Edwards to initiate the type's extensive flight-test activities. Another five FSD F-111B aircraft would be evaluated by the U.S. Navy at its fight-test base located at Naval Air Station, Patuxent River, Maryland.

The second of two North American XB-70A
continued on page 118

Robert K. "Bob" Parsons, Colonel USAF (Retired)

Bob Parsons, now an environmental lawyer for the state of West Virginia, retired from the USAF in 1978 after serving for twenty-six-and-a-half years. He was at Edwards from late-1961 to mid-1969 and, among other duties, he performed stability and control testing on the McDonnell Douglas F-4 Phantom 2, the Northrop F-5 Freedom Fighter, and all models of the General Dynamics F-111. After leaving Edwards, "Bobcat," Parsons' call sign, flew 175 combat missions in the North American F100 Super Sabre and another ten combat sorties in the British-built Canberra bomber.

The following letter was written to the author on March 26, 1993. According to Parsons, the phrases "nickel-and-dime" and "cats and dogs," mean "miscellaneous."

"After graduating from the experimental test pilot course at the Aerospace Research Pilot School [now Test Pilot School] at Edwards AFB in 1962, some of us stayed on and completed what was then referred to as 'Space Class IV.' After graduating from the Space Class, we were assigned to the Fighter Test Section at Edwards and initially participated in several Apollo simulation missions with Martin Marietta in Baltimore, Maryland, while, at the time, conducting many 'nickel-and-dime' tests primarily on COIN [counter-insurgency] airplanes, such as the YAT-26, YAT-28, and YAT-37, and various other tests of this type.

"The first major program I was assigned to was stability and control test pilot for the Northrop F-5 Freedom Fighter under the International Fighter Program. This fighter was a derivative of the Northrop T-38 Talon trainer. The F-5 was primarily produced as a single-seat and a two-seat version, to include a reconnaissance version. These low-cost, relatively high-performance fighters were purchased by many NATO [North Atlantic Treaty Organization] countries. After performing many of the stability tests, to include various external store loadings, we discussed with the Northrop engineers innovative ways to investigate out-of-control situations and whether a spin test was necessary.

"The consensus of the operational pilots and various test pilots was that a spin program really did not tell you much about the airplane. What you really want to know was, If the airplane became uncontrollable, what was the best recovery technique for the pilot to apply, other than ejecting from the airplane? To this end, various operational maneuvers were discussed and certain ones were selected to be demonstrated with the spin-configured F-5 airplane. This airplane, of course, had a spin recovery parachute and additional pilot restraints due to the excessive motion that we predicted would occur in the cockpit. Generally, the airplane was extremely difficult to maneuver into uncontrollable flight. After much experimenting, the best recovery method was basically to take your hands off the controls and the airplane would recover if there was sufficient altitude.

"One of the maneuvers selected for testing involved pulling the airplane into a vertical attitude so that it was going straight up, holding this position until the air speed decreased to 100 knots, and then immediately pulling the stick full back and holding it for two seconds. One could certainly question the sanity of an operational pilot who would perform such a maneuver, but we reasoned that somebody might—and I was selected to test this maneuver.

"In preparing for this flight, we ran the maneuver on the simulator, and it showed that nothing would happen, that the airplane would flop on its back, roll over once or twice, and then recover. Of course, we were being tracked by cameras and had all types of instrumentation installed. We began the run at about 30,000ft, obtained a speed of a little in excess of 1.1 Mach number, then rotated the airplane vertical. With the airplane vertical, going through approximately 40,000ft with the air speed decreasing through 100 knots, I abruptly, with both hands, pulled full aft stick as hard and as fast as I could and held it for 'one-thousand-one, one-thousand-two' counts. The airplane responded very crisply and flopped over on its back with the air speed now being something less than the air speed indicator would record. I released the control stick forces and expected the airplane to either roll over or go into an inverted spin. However, it did nothing. The F-5 fell from about 40,000ft to 20,000ft on its back without moving. It was rather eerie. The engines were at idle, one flamed out, and the people on the ground, of course, had the safety task that if I was not recovered by 15,000ft they were to start the bailout warning. As the airplane fell upside down it did not roll or yaw; it was very quiet. The F-5 had absolutely no discernible motion except falling. As I went through 20,000ft, the airplane, for some reason, went a little more nose--down, still inverted, and shook so vigorously that I could not read the instrument panel. Then, the F-5 flopped upright, and it was just a matter of recovering the airplane for normal flight. We did have external photographs, and it was just uncanny how the airplane fell on its back without being disrupted by anything. That flight was part of the fun of spin testing.

Parsons in a Lockheed F-104.

"One other instance which happened while testing the General Dynamics F-111 has remained with me for years. I flew many early flights out of General Dynamics' facility at Fort Worth, Texas, and was accompanied on most of them by great professional General Dynamics engineers in the right seat to manage the various data systems which recorded our testing parameters. One particular engineer was an outstanding engineer but slightly nervous if anything out of the ordinary went on during the test flight.

"The early F-111s had notoriously inaccurate and erratic engine oil pressure gauges. One or the other would start vibrating or go to zero after about twenty minutes of flight. We aborted some early flights because of this malfunction. However, in every check we made of the system, there was nothing wrong with the engine oil pressure; it was always the gauges.

"On one of the first ferry flights of the prototype F-111 from Fort Worth to Edwards, the General Dynamics engineer and I were to fly the airplane to Edwards and cruise at about 27,000ft with a chase airplane, which happened to be a General Dynamics F-106 Delta Dart. The chase pilot maintained radio contact with us. We were collecting certain test data along the route from a performance standpoint, and, as we approached El Paso, Texas, one of our engine oil pressure gauges started fluctuating wildly from zero to maximum. The engineer became preoccupied with it, and I came prepared [for his reaction]. I took a piece of masking tape I had brought along for the occasion and taped over the gauge. This seemed to settle him down a little bit since he could not see the gauge. Within another five minutes, we had passed over El Paso, when the other gauge started fluctuating. I put masking tape over that gauge as well, and the engineer was again satisfied. I was feeling smug at the time when suddenly there was something like a burp from a baby and both engines flamed out. The engineer looked at me, and I looked at the engineer. We called our chase plane and sank toward the ground very briskly. There were certain things in the early F-111s that you had to do because of the test instrumentation before you could restart the engines. It seemed like it took us an eternity to do these tasks. Once we got them completed, we restarted both engines. They started back up just fine. The chase pilot had rejoined us by then. He saw no smoke, no fire, and, to make a happy ending to the story, we proceeded to Edwards because we could find nothing wrong with the airplane that would require an emergency landing en route. Once we got on the ground and the engines were given a thorough check, it was again the engine oil gauges themselves that had malfunctioned. After that incident, I always wondered why that particular General Dynamics engineer was not too keen on flying with me on any more tests.

"Another F-111 story that stands out in my mind is the first supersonic automatic terrain-following flight—i.e. hands off, auto-pilot run of the F-111 at supersonic speed at 200ft above the ground. This test took a lot of preparation. We had to get permission from the FAA [Federal Aviation Administration], the state of Califor-

nia, and the state of Nevada to lay out a route that was 200mi long over which we could fly the F-111 at supersonic speeds within 200ft of the ground. The route selected was to fly north in an isolated valley that generally ran parallel to Death Valley on the east and Owens Valley on the west. This route of flight only crossed one secondary California highway which did not have very heavy traffic, especially in the morning. We had made arrangements with the sheriff and highway patrol responsible for this area to block traffic the morning of our first supersonic attempt. We also had various cameras positioned along the flight path on the top of the mountain ridges to record the flight.

"Perhaps, you have seen this flight. Anytime there are documentaries on the F-111, they show the flight with the airplane coming up the valley and the rooster tail or supersonic shock clearly visible behind the airplane.

"Our speed on the first run was to be a little greater than 1.2 Mach number. As you know, at sea level, this Mach number is in excess of 800mph. We had a chase plane that was to join us and check us over after the first 100mi of the run. As we descended into the valley floor and turned on the terrain-following radar and the auto-pilot, we leveled out at about 150ft above the desert at about 800mph. The automatic terrain-following radar fluctuated slightly so that our actual altitude over the ground varied between 90 and 250ft. As we approached the secondary highway at a 90deg angle, we could see a Winnebago motor home and two police cars, but it was too late—we were over them and gone. We pulled up and slowed down, and our chase plane joined us. We were very concerned about what the shock wave may have done to the Winnebago camper. After landing back at Edwards, we talked with the highway patrolmen. They were unable to stop the elderly couple in the Winnebago and get them out of there before we came over. However, they did say that the couple really liked the air show and that there was no damage to their recreational vehicle.

"Fortunatel for the F-111 program, this convinced the state authorities that we should not have any problem running supersonically over the route we had proposed. As a postscript, the chase pilot had checked the F-111 over and had said we looked good. He then departed the area. Prior to getting out of the airplane, we noticed the plane's crew chief making signals to shut the engines off. We shut them down very quickly and exited the airplane. We followed the crew chief to the back of the airplane, and there were two panels approximately 4ft by 15ft long that had just literally disappeared from the airplane [these were the engine access panels underneath the airplane], possibly from the vibration of the supersonic, low-level flight. We must have lost these after our chase pilot had departed the area—he surely would have noticed these huge covers missing; the engine access panels were never found.

"In closing, as you can probably surmise, all the 'cats and dogs' testing of fighters and other aircraft at Edwards created a lot of fun times."

Paul F. Bikle (center, dark suit), director of NASA's Dryden Flight Research Facility from 1959 to 1971, meets with six of the twelve pilots who flew the X-15 during its nine-year flight-test program. The pilots are, from left to right, USAF Maj. Joe Engle, NASA's Milt Thompson, USAF majors Robert Rushworth and Pete Knight, and

NASA pilots John McKay and Bill Dana. The six others who flew the X-15 were Scott Crossfield (North American Aviation), NASA pilots Joe Walker and Neil Armstrong (first man to walk on the moon), USAF majors Robert White and Michael Adams, and USN Lt. Cmdr. Forrest Petersen. NASA

continued from page 15
Valkyrie research aircraft arrived at Edwards on July 17, following its maiden flight from Palmdale. Once again, North American's Al White was the pilot and the USAF's Col. Joe Cotton was the copilot.

On October 14, during its seventeenth flight, XB-70A number one made its first triple-sonic-speed flight when it attained 3.02 Mach number at 70,000ft. This was the first time in history that a bomber-sized airplane had flown at such a high speed; and, except for Bell's X-2, North American's X-15, and Lockheed's Blackbird series of aircraft (A-12/F-12/SR-71), it was the highest speed flown by a manned air vehicle. On January 3, 1966, coincidentally during its seventeenth flight, XB-70A number two matched its sister ship's performance

with a flight to 3.05 Mach number at 72,000ft. In both cases, White was the pilot and Cotton was the copilot.

Right
After making first flights at Convair's Fort Worth, Texas, facility, a number of B-58A Hustlers were ferried to Edwards for additional testing. An early-production B-58A poses here with a General Electric J79 turbojet engine, which allowed the type to dash to speeds beyond 2 Mach number, and created the world's first double-sonic bomber airplane. It was a B-58A like this that allowed USAF Maj. "Fitz" Fulton to reach 85,360ft with an 11,023lb payload on September 18, 1962—a record that still stands. General Electric

1966

As mentioned earlier, Major General Branch died in a plane crash on January 3, 1966. His deputy commander, Col. Ray Vandiver temporarily commanded the AFFTC until January 17, when Maj. Gen. High B. Manson took over. Manson remained as base commander until December 6, 1968.

The XB-70A continued to impress. The highest speed attained by either of the two examples occurred on April 12, 1966, when XB-70A number two flew at 3.08 Mach number at 72,800ft, again, with White and Cotton at the controls. The highest flight, to 74,000ft (14mi), had been flown on March 19 with the same airplane. In that instance, White was pilot and North American's Van H. Shepard—White's backup on the B-70 program—was copilot.

What has been called "the blackest day in the history of Edwards AFB" took place on June 8, 1966. After a series of tests, XB-70A number two joined up with four jet aircraft, also powered by General Electric jet engines, for an information public relations photo session near the base. One of the jet airplanes in the formation, a NASA F-104N flown by NASA's Joe Walker, collided in mid-air with the lowered right wingtip of the Valkyrie. The F-104N rolled inverted up and over the top of the XB-70A, shearing off all of its right vertical tail and most of its left vertical tail. It then pounded at the top of the Valkyrie's left wing before exploding, disintegrating, and falling to the desert floor. The XB-70A, behaving as if nothing had happened, flew straight and level for about sixteen seconds before it began losing altitude. Pilot Al White was able to eject on the way down; he suffered severe injuries but survived. His copilot, USAF Maj. Carl S. Cross, who was on his first XB-70A flight, did not eject and rode the plane to his death. NASA's Joe Walker was also killed in this tragic collision.

The Northrop-built M2-F2 wingless lifting body air vehicle was the follow-on to the NASA-

An early F-4C (formerly F-110A) Phantom 2 at Edwards during flight-test activities. Originally developed and produced for the U.S. Navy, the U.S. Air Force be- *came the Phantom 2's biggest customer. It's rare indeed when the USAF adopts a USN fighter, or vice versa.* USAF via AFFTC/HO

built M2-F1 wingless lifting body. The M2-F2 made its first glide flight at Edwards on July 12, followed by a series of powered flights until it crash landed on Rogers Dry Lake on May 10, 1967. NASA's Bruce Peterson, though badly injured, recovered. The seriously damaged M2-F2 was rebuilt as the M2-F3, and NASA's and the USAF's studies into the flight of lifting body shapes without wings continued.

The Northrop HL-10 lifting body, one of four wingless air vehicles flown during the late-1960s at Edwards by NASA's Dryden Flight Research Facility, made its first glide flight on December 22, 1966. The HL-10's best marks for altitude and

The M2-F1 lightweight lifting body lowers to land during one of the more than 100 flights it made between August 1963 and August 1964. The one-of-a-kind powerless air vehicle, built of plywood over a tubular steel frame, pioneered the concept of maneuverable flight with conventional wings. The subsequent fleet of heavier, powered lifting bodies were flown from 1966 to 1975 and helped in the development of the space shuttles. NASA pilot Milt Thompson was first to fly the M2-F1. It was first tested while being towed behind an automobile over Rogers Dry Lake. It was later towed into the air behind a NASA C-47 to altitudes of about 10,000ft for a series of unpowered flights back to the lake bed. NASA

The number three NF-104A now resides alongside the USAF Test Pilot School at Edwards AFB. USAF via AFFTC/HO

speed are 90,303ft (17.1mi) with NASA pilot Bill Dana, and 1.86 Mach number with USAF pilot Pete Hoag; these marks occurred on February 18 and 27, 1970, respectively.

1967

The first U-2R—an advanced version of the U-2 series—made its premier flight on August 28, 1967, at Edwards' secretive North Base; it was piloted by Lockheed test pilot Bill Park.

Left
The number one NF-104A zoomed upward from Edwards AFB on its first flight in late-1963. Its tail-mounted rocket motor is at full thrust—6,000lb; note the stabilator deflection. Lockheed

On October 3, 1967 the X-15 achieved its highest speed. On that day, piloting the X-15A-2, USAF Maj. William J. "Pete" Knight shot to a speed of 6.7 Mach number (4,520mph). To this writing, the speed attained on that flight remains the fastest that any man has ever flown in an airplane.

1968

The 199th and last flight in the very successful North American, USAF, NASA, and Navy X-15A/X-15A-2 flight-test program occurred October 24, 1968, with NASA's William H. "Bill" Dana at the controls. It was not until the advent of the Grumman X-29A that an X-plane surpassed the X-15's record number of flights. The X-15 was the

123

The one-of-a-kind Ryan XV-5A Vertifan hovers just prior to a vertical landing at Edwards. The XV-5A used fuselage-mounted jet engines to drive three large-diameter fans mounted in the wings (two) and the nose (one) for liftoff, hovering, and landing. Jet thrust was used for

horizontal flight. Conceived in 1955 and tested extensively in 1964–1965, the XV-5A was turned over to NASA (tail number 705) for further vertical takeoff and landing (VTOL) research. Teledyne Ryan Aeronautical

first airplane to fly above 200,000 and 300,000ft and the first to fly beyond four, five, and six times the speed of sound. Its best altitude and speed marks, 67-plus miles and 6.7 Mach number, still stand. Only the space shuttles and space capsules returning from earth orbit have surpassed the X-15's speed and altitude marks.

On December 7, 1968, USAF Brig. Gen. Alton D. Slay, who would later be instrumental in the development of the F-117 stealth fighter, became base commander; he served until July 31, 1970.

1969

Following eighty-two flights, the surviving number one XB-70A Valkyrie departed Edwards AFB on February 4, 1969, to join the U.S. Air Force Museum's collection of historic air vehicles. Its eighty-third flight, from Edwards to Wright-Patterson AFB, Dayton, Ohio, where the Air Force Museum is located, was flown by NASA's Fitz Ful-

ton, pilot, and USAF Lt. Col. Ted Sturmthal, copilot. The two XB-70As flew a total of 128 flights. Although only one-hour forty-eight minutes of the total flight time was spent at Mach 3 number or above, no other air vehicle in the weight class of the Valkyrie (500,000lb) has exceeded three times the speed of sound.

On April 17, the fifth wingless lifting body, flown by the USAF's Jerauld Gentry, made its first and successful glide flight at Edwards. Built by Martin-Marietta, it was designated X-24A.

The first C-5A Galaxy was ferried to Edwards for ongoing evaluations after its first flight at Lockheed's Marietta, Georgia, facility on June 30, 1968. On October 14, 1969, it set a world takeoff weight record of 789,200lb. With that hallmark event, the 1960s and its dynamic events drew to a close at Edwards AFB.

Records set in 1969 included an unofficial world class speed record of 6.7 Mach number (4,520 mph) and an unofficial world-class altitude record of 67.08mi (354,200ft) by a rocket-powered air vehicle.

While the 1950s had been a decade of aeronautical learning, the 1960s had been a decade of astounding aerospace progress. Truly, the advances in aeronautics and astronautics that were made in the 1960s at Edwards AFB were unparalleled in the annals of aviation history.

In addition, as had been the case in the two preceding decades, several advanced types of aircraft had materialized and moved into production. These were:

- McDonnell F-4 and RF-4 Phantom II
- Northrop F-5 Freedom Fighter
- General Dynamics F-111
- Lockheed C-5 Galaxy
- Douglas DC-9

Although the 1960s at Edwards AFB did not nurture an entirely new type of production aircraft, it truly was a decade of higher speeds and higher altitudes. The 1970s, armed with the technological advances made in the 1960s, would bring forth a new breed of fighter aircraft blessed with unheard-of maneuverability and agility.

This is why America successfully landed and took off from the moon six times during the Apollo program. NASA pilot Neil A. Armstrong—first man to walk on the moon—flies the number two lunar landing research vehicle (LLRV) during test flights at Edwards between 1964 and 1966. Built by Bell Aerospace Textron, the LLRV was powered by a 4,200lb thrust turbofan engine and a group of hydrogen peroxide rockets. The twelve men that walked on the moon owe their success, in part, to this ungainly looking contraption. NASA

The first of two XB-70As flies at about 0.95Mn with its wingtips lowered to their mid-down (25deg) deflection. Affectionately nicknamed the Great White Bird, the XB-70A was the world's first, and still only, tri-sonic bomber-type airplane. Before it was retired to the U.S. Air Force Museum, XB-70A number one flew eighty-three times from 1964 to 1969. The XB-70A's chase plane, a TB-58A, flies alongside in a 2Mn versus 3Mn bomber speed duel. USAF via Tony Landis

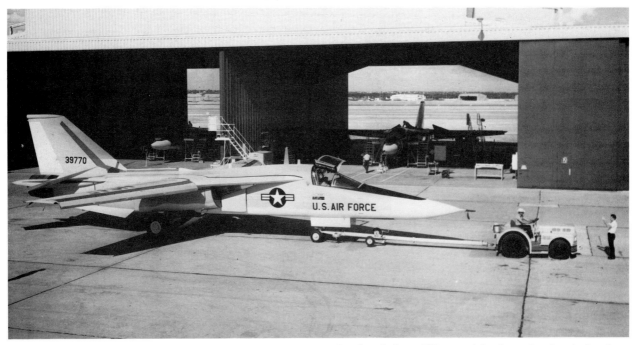

Developed as an advanced tactical fighter in the 1960s, the General Dynamics F-111, an exceptional warplane, was extensively tested at Edwards by USAF test pilot Robert K. "Bob" Parsons and others. After years of "do we need this airplane?" controversy, the answer came loud and clear: "We certainly do and we're glad to have it!" While two other F-111As are serviced in their hangers, F-111A number five is towed out for yet another test flight, circa 1965. General Dynamics

The premier Douglas DC-9 twinjet jetliner flies to Edwards from Long Beach. It competed with Boeing's 737.
McDonnell Douglas via Mike Machat Illustration

The number one YF-12A automatically compensates center of gravity over Edwards by dumping fuel prior to one of many landings there. Derived from the A-12, which led to the SR-71, the F-12 was likely the best interceptor ever produced. USAF via Jim Goodall and Tony Landis

The number two XB-70A shows off its half-airplane/half-spaceship lines while banking left over Edwards. Valkyrie, powered by six 30,000lb-thrust class General Electric J93 turbojet engines, featured a vari-able-geometry windshield ramp and fold-down wingtips for improved aerodynamics at 3Mn speed. XB-70A number two flew forty-six times. USAF via Tony Landis

Joe Walker's NASA F-104 moves too close under the right wing of XB-70A number two just prior to the tragic mid-air collision on June 8, 1966, which caused the loss of two pilots and two planes. The collision occurred mo- *ments after this photograph was taken and, several minutes later, both planes crashed to the desert floor below.* USAF via Tom Rosquin

The landing gear on NASA's B-52A begins folding back into the fuselage as the airplane climbs to altitude with the M2-F2 lifting body suspended from its wing pylon mount. This was one of two B-52s modified to air-launch lifting bodies and X-15 research aircraft in the 1960s. This B-52 was nicknamed The High and Mighty Two. NASA

The M2-F3 lifting body, suspended from its B-52 carrier airplane, nears launch altitude on one of its research flights at Edwards. Lifting bodies were air-launched from the B-52 and used rocket motors to reach planned altitudes and speeds. The approach-and-landing phases of the flights were powerless. NASA

The Northrop HL-10 lifting body, posing on the surface of Rogers Dry Lake, flew the fastest (1,228mph) and the highest (90,030ft) in the wingless lifting body program. The program helped produce energy management data and landing techniques now used by space shuttle pilots. Other lifting body designs were the M2-F2, M2-F3 (rebuilt M2-F2 following a landing accident), X-24A, and X-24B (rebuilt X-24A with different configuration). An earlier plywood lifting body, the M2-F1, validated basic lifting body stability and control characteristics and paved the way for the formal "heavyweight" program, which resulted in the HL-10 and its counterpart vehicles. NASA

A Lockheed U-2R on a flight test out of Edwards AFB's North Base glides over the Tehachapi Mountains to the west. The success of the U-2R, a redesigned version of earlier model U-2s, led to Lockheed's creation of the TR-1 (Tactical Reconnaissance One) aircraft. Today, to avoid confusion, the TR-1 aircraft have been redesignated U-2R. Lockheed

The Martin-Marietta X-24A lifting body poses on a ramp at NASA's Flight Research Facility at Edwards AFB. The X-24A was later rebuilt as the X-24B. Before rebuild, the X-24A flew twenty-eight times from April 1969 to June 1971. It was flown by one NASA pilot and two USAF pilots. NASA

Chapter 4

Class Acts
The 1970s

We [Muroc AAF personnel in the early-1940s] couldn't get a commanding officer.
Commissioned officers would come up from Los Angeles, take one look at the place, and
take off for L.A. again without even shutting off the motors of their airplanes.
—MSgt. Harley J. Fogelman

It generally takes a long, long time to advance the so-called state-of-the-art, especially in the technological realms of aeronautics and astronautics. Still, the 1960s at Edwards AFB saw countless aero-/astro-technological advancements realized. Truly, the men and women at Edwards AFB had overcome the impossible by accomplishing the

incredible. For example, manned air vehicles air-launched by mother ships had blasted past six-and-one-half times the speed of sound and had rocketed above 67mi. Subsequently in the 1970s, with the arrivals of advanced attack, bomber, fighter, and research aircraft, the stage at Edwards presented a series of class acts.

Three of the five so-called "heavyweight" wingless lifting bodies pose side by side on Rogers Dry Lake. From left, they are the X-24A, M2-F3, and HL-10. These air vehicles were flown from July 1966 to November 1975 to in- *vestigate the feasibility of maneuvering and landing an aerodynamic craft designed for reentry from space.* NASA

1970

The 1970s at Edwards AFB began with ongoing USAF/NASA research into wingless lifting body air vehicles.

On February 18, 1970, with USAF Maj. Pete Hoag on board, the rocket-powered Northrop HL-10 hit 1.86 Mach number at 67,310ft, the highest speed that would be attained throughout the lifting body test program.

The lifting body air vehicles were designed and tested to determine whether wingless body shapes could make precise landings after gliding descents from high altitudes. They pioneered many of the approach-and-landing techniques that were later employed by the space shuttles.

The feasibility of the lifting body air vehicle design was further proven on February 27, when NASA test pilot Bill Dana piloted the HL-10 to an altitude of 90,303ft (17.1mi), then made a successful, powerless descent to a deadstick landing on Rogers Dry Lake. The altitude attained during this flight was the highest recorded throughout the multi-phase lifting body test program.

Lifting body research, begun with the M2/F1 and M2/F2, continued well into the 1970s with the HL-10, X-24A, M2/F3, and the X-24B all participating.

Powered by a single 8,480lb-thrust rocket motor, the X-24A made its first powered flight on March 19 with the USAF's Jerauld Gentry in control. The X-24A had accomplished nine unpowered flights and this time, it was flown out to a speed of 0.865 Mach number (571mph) and 44,384ft.

On August 1, now-Brig. Gen. Robert M. White—first pilot to exceed 4, 5, and 6 Mach numbers—became base commander, a position he held until October 18, 1972.

The premier DC-10 jetliner, after its first take-off from Douglas' Long Beach facility, made its first landing at Edwards AFB on August 29, 1970,

The Martin Marietta X-24B used the cockpit, engine, basic structures, and subsystems of the bulb-shaped X-24A. The main difference was its new exterior structure which gave it a delta shape that doubled its lifting surface. The X-24A's ability to maneuver some 1,000mi on either side of its flight path increased nearly three-fold with the X-24B because of its improved aerodynamic shape. It featured a triangular cross section, flat bottom, rounded top, and double delta planform with three vertical fins. NASA

The premier McDonnell Douglas DC-10 flies over Edwards during another certification flight. A tri-jet, the DC-10 competed with Boeing's 747; it is no longer in production. McDonnell Douglas via Mike Machat Illustration

for ongoing tests. It was piloted by Clifford L. Stout.

1971

With NASA's John Manke at the controls, the last powered flight on the X-24A lifting body air vehicle was made on June 4, 1971. And after twenty-eight total flights (unpowered and powered), the aircraft had flown just two hours, fifty-four minutes, and twenty-eight seconds. Its highest speed was 1.60 Mach number, and its highest altitude was 71,400ft.

The third of three Lockheed YF-12As was lost at Edwards on June 24, 1971. An in-flight fire that could not be extinguished forced its USAF crew to eject from the burning aircraft. Prior to its loss, this particular YF-12A had flown 198 times, accumulating 449.8 flying hours.

On December 20, 1971, the USAF Aerospace Research Pilot School completed the final flight on one of its two remaining NF-104A aircraft. After

retirement, NF-104A number one was put on display atop a pylon outside the USAF Test Pilot School. USAF ARPS became USAF TPS on July 1, 1972.

1972

Following its arrival from Republic Aviation's facility at Farmingdale, Long Island, New York, the first service-test YA-10A Thunderbolt II airplane, nicknamed *Warthog,* made a successful first

Right
The third of three service-test Lockheed YF-12A Improved Manned Interceptors flies at high altitude near Edwards AFB prior to its June 24, 1971, crash following an in-flight fire. It has been said—and there is no reason to doubt it—that the F-12 was the best all-missile-armed, all-weather interceptor airplane ever built. As luck would have it, though, a lack of funding doomed it before a full-production version, the proposed F-12B, could be procured. Lockheed

Northrop built two service-test YA-9A attack aircraft to compete with Republic's two YA-10As. Although similar, as far as mission requirements dictated, the Northrop YA-9A was defeated by Republic's YA-10A in January 1973 after a close fly-off competition at Edwards. The first of two YA-9As is shown. USAF via AFFTC/HO

The first of two Republic YA-10A service-test airplanes carries six Maverick television-guided, air-to-ground missiles during weapons testing at Edwards, circa 1972. Armed with a single nose-mounted 30mm GAU-8/A cannon with 1,350 rounds of armor-piercing ammuni-tion, the A-10 can also carry up to 16,000lb of mixed ordnance on eleven hard points. The A-10, after a fly-off with Northrop's YA-9A, was ordered into production in March 1973; 720 were built. USAF via AFFTC/HO

A relatively close-up view of South Base and the entire 15,000ft runway complex at Edwards. The runway com- *plex, completed in October 1954, was then the longest concrete runway in the USAF.* USAF via AFFTC/HO

flight at Edwards AFB on May 10, 1972. It was to participate in a fly-off competition with the Northrop YA-9A, which on May 30 made its first successful flight at Edwards after its arrival from Northrop's Hawthorne facility. Ultimately, Republic's A-10 prevailed.

After its rollout at St. Louis on June 26, 1972, the first McDonnell Aircraft F-15A Eagle arrived at Edwards via a C-5A transport. On July 27, with McDonnell chief test pilot Irving L. "Irv" Burrows at the controls, it made a successful first flight of fifty minutes. During this test, he flew what was to become the best air superiority fighter in the world to an altitude of 12,000ft and a speed of 320mph. Thirteen months later, the type had exceeded 60,000ft and 2.5 Mach number.

USAF Brig. Gen. Howard M. Lane became base commander on October 18, 1972; he commanded until February 24, 1974.

During 1971 and 1972, NASA flew a number of flight-test missions on a pair of modified USN F-8 Crusaders. First to fly, NASA number 810 was

an F-8A modified to investigate the NASA-developed Supercritical Wing; second to fly, NASA number 802 was an F-8C modified to investigate a Digital Fly-by-Wire Flight Control System. Both aircraft performed flawlessly during subsequent years, and today, after their respective retirements, they are displayed together outside NASA's facility at Edwards AFB.

1973–1974

After the USAF/NASA X-24A had been rebuilt as the X-24B, NASA's John Manke made its first unpowered glide flight on August 1, 1973. Its first powered flight, again with Manke in control, was on November 15, 1973. After thirty-six total flights (unpowered and powered), ending on September 9, 1975, the X-24B had achieved 1.76 Mach number, 74,130ft altitude, and a total flying time of three-hours, forty-six minutes, and 43.6 seconds.

On January 21, 1974, the first of two service-test YF-16 lightweight fighters completed an unscheduled six-minute first flight with General Dy-

The first pre-production McDonnell Douglas F-15 Eagle soars above Edwards AFB in late-1972. The F-15 was the first U.S. airplane to be operational with engine thrust exceeding its loaded weight, thus permitting it to accelerate while in a vertical climb. In fact, it was the first airplane to exceed Mach one while climbing straight up. Production F-15s (A, B, C, and D models) are all-weather, highly maneuverable, double-sonic-plus tactical fighters that can gain and maintain air superiority in aerial combat, and can out-fight and out-perform any current enemy fighter. McDonnell Douglas

The first supercritical wing to be flight tested on an aircraft—NASA F-8A, tail number 810—appears as a graceful extension to the upper fuselage of this modified Crusader. It was flown by NASA's Ames/Dryden Flight Research Facility at Edwards AFB from 1971 to 1973. The wing, developed at NASA's Langley Research Center by Richard Whitcomb, features an airfoil that is flatter on top and more rounded on the bottom than conventional airfoils. Research flights with the wing showed that the supercritical airfoil delayed the formation of the shock wave over the wing at high subsonic speeds, resulting in less drag. This allowed the airplane to cruise farther and faster, with increased payloads and greater fuel efficiency. Many military and civilian aircraft are now flying with this wing type. NASA

NASA's F-8C (tail number 802) Digital Fly-by-Wire research airplane cruises over Edwards AFB on one of its pioneering flights in the 1970s. NASA's research developed the computerized fly-by-wire flight control systems used in many aircraft today. The F-8C's conventional flight control system was replaced with a digital electronic system utilizing a computer from an Apollo space-craft. The first flight of the DFBW F-8C was May 25, 1972, by NASA's Gary Krier. After initial flight-test activities were completed, the DFBW F-8C was used to test the prototype fly-by-wire sidestick system in the F-16, and later, tested the computer software for the space shuttle's digital flight control system. The F-8C shown was retired from flight status in 1985. NASA

namics' Philip F. "Phil" Oestricher at the controls. As it came about, during a high-speed taxi to check nose wheel steering, brakes, and so on, the airplane began to rock from side to side violently. Instead of riding it out on the ground, where more damage might occur (the right stabilator—combined stabilizer and elevator—had already been damaged), Oestricher opted to take off, circle, and land as soon as he could. The minor damage was repaired and the airplane was cleared for flight.

Phil Oestricher took the repaired YF-16 on a successful, and official, first flight of ninety min-utes on February 2, 1974. , General Dynamics test pilot Neil A. Anderson accomplished the first flight on YF-16 number two on May 9.

USAF Maj. Gen. Robert A. Rushworth, who had flown thirty-four X-15 flights (the most of any-one), was named base commander on February 25, 1974, and held the post until November 3, 1975.

The number one Northrop YF-17 service-test lightweight fighter was trucked to Edwards from Hawthorne, then piloted on its maiden flight by Northrop test pilot Henry E. "Hank" Chouteau on June 9, 1974. The flight lasted sixty-one minutes, and a top speed of 610mph was reached at a peak altitude of 18,000ft.

An amazing thing happened at Edwards on June 23, 1974. For the first time in aviation history, a turbojet-only-powered airplane—specifically the number one YF-17—attained supersonic speed in level attitude flight without the use of afterburning. This was a prelude to today's supercruise feature of advanced tactical fighters, whereby supersonic cruise is a standard practice without afterburners.

Later that summer, the number two service-test YF-17 made a successful first flight on August 21, 1974. Hank Chouteau was at the controls during the sixty-one minute flight, during which a peak altitude of 27,000ft and a top speed of

A service-test General Dynamics YF-16 Fighting Falcon, equipped with two wingtip-mounted Sidewinders and two underwing-mounted Sparrows, flies near Edwards AFB. Although the YF-16 beat Northrop's YF-17 in the USAF Lightweight Fighter competition, the latter proved successful later when it reemerged as the McDonnell Douglas/Northrop F/A-18 Hornet for the USN and USMC. The F-16 was the world's first operational airplane with a digital fly-by-wire flight control system. General Dynamics

615mph were attained. Thus was launched the competition between the Fighting Falcon, as the F-16 was named, and the Cobra, as the F-17 was named.

Following a one-hour and eighteen-minute shakedown flight from Palmdale, Charles C. "Charlie" Bock Jr., chief test pilot for Rockwell's B-1 Division, landed the premier swing-wing Rockwell B-1A bomber at Edwards on December 23, 1974. This airplane, forerunner of today's fleet of B-1B Lancers, was later joined by three more B-1As for flight test and evaluation.

1975–1976

Earlier, on August 5, 1975, in a fine demonstration of the lifting body program, NASA test pilot John Manke brought the rocket-powered X-24B in for a near-perfect landing on Edwards' main concrete runway after an unpowered descent from 57,050ft. This was the first time a landing, within the limited confines of a conventional concrete runway, had been attempted. Along with a subsequent flight by USAF Maj. Michael Love, it demonstrated that these unconventional, wingless lifting body shapes could, truly, make precise landings on runways, whereby touchdown accuracy of plus-or-minus 500ft could be attained. All these lifting body tests came to fruition two years later.

On August 26, 1975, following a two hour and twenty-six minute flight from Long Beach, the number one McDonnell Douglas YC-15 Advanced Medium STOL (short takeoff and landing) Transport or AMST airplane landed at Edwards.

Famed General Dynamics test pilots Neil R. Anderson (cockpit) and Philip F. "Phil" Oestricher (ladder) discuss a flight test of the second of two YF-16s at Edwards, circa 1975. Prior to the F-16 program, Anderson flew seven years on the F-111 flight-test program. Oestricher, also heavily involved in the F-111 program, was F-16 project pilot, and in 1990 became director of flight test for General Dynamics' Fort Worth Division in Texas. General Dynamics

143

The first of two Northrop service-test YF-17 Cobra light-weight fighters banks toward Rogers Dry Lake during its first flight. On a later flight test, without the use of its afterburners, the YF-17 became the world's first fighter-type to exceed Mach one in level-attitude flight! Even though the YF-17 lost out to the YF-16, it was too good of a design to forget. Thus, after redesign, it was produced as the USN's and the USMC's F/A-18 Hornet. As the F/A-18, it remains in production at this writing. USAF via General Electric

For comparison, the number one YF-17 (foreground) is parked next to the number two YF-16. USAF via AFFTC/HO

The Rockwell B-1A was the winner of the USAF's AMSA (Advanced Manned Strategic Aircraft) competition and the forerunner of today's B-1B Lancer. Powered by four 30,000lb-thrust class turbojets, the B-1A was capable of Mach two-plus speeds. The B-1B, however, is limited to 1.25 Mach number. Rockwell via Chris Wamsley

The YC-15 AMST aircraft was intended to compete with two Boeing YC-14 AMST aircraft in a winner-take-all competition for AMST production rights. Boeing's entry was to follow about one year later and, after the fly-off, the winner of the competition would be announced.

Base command changed hands November 4, 1975, with USAF Maj. Gen. Thomas P. Stafford taking the reins as commander of the AFFTC; he commanded until March 7, 1978.

The number three B-1A prototype made its first flight from Palmdale to Edwards AFB, where it joined B-1A number one on April 1, 1976. During its four-hour, fifty-four minute maiden flight, it attained a speed of about 630mph (0.85 Mach number) at 15,000ft. The number three B-1A flew before B-1A number two because the second B-1A spent eight months in static structural airframe tests at Palmdale prior to its first flight (June 14, 1976, from Palmdale to Edwards).

Following a number of flight tests out of Boeing field in Seattle, the number one YC-14 AMST prototype arrived at Edwards to challenge the YC-15s on November 9, 1976. It was followed two days later, by Boeing's number two YC-14 AMST prototype.

1977–1979

NASA's space shuttle era commenced August

12, 1977, when, the space shuttle *Enterprise*, named after the *Starship Enterprise* in the "Star Trek" television series, was launched from the back of a 747 carrier airplane at 24,100ft and successfully completed a five-minute twenty-one-second descent to a landing and rollout on Rogers Dry Lake. (The *Enterprise* was a non-orbiting craft built to confirm the space shuttle design's low-speed airworthiness during unpowered approach-and-landing (ALT) tests prior to actual orbital flights by subsequent shuttles.) This and four additional ALT tests demonstrated the soundness of the shuttle design and confirmed the approach-and-landing techniques that would later be used by shuttle pilots returning from Earth-orbiting missions.

The AMST fly-off competition ended in 1977; the YC-14 had made 369 flights, while the YC-15 had completed 332 flights. However, due to budgetary restrictions at the time, no winner was named and the AMST program was terminated.

Although both types of AMST aircraft had performed as advertised, neither type "won" and all four service-test aircraft were placed in long-term storage. Although Boeing's YC-14 design was probably more innovative, the fact that McDonnell Douglas' YC-15 could match its performance with less power and had the added safety of four engines, undoubtedly impressed the decision board. The evidence for this lies in the fact that McDonnell Douglas' C-17, based on its earlier YC-15 design, won the follow-on Advanced Heavy-lift STOL Transport (AHST) competition. Incidentally, the C-17's closest rival was Boeing's AHST entry, which was based on its earlier YC-14 design.

USAF Brig. Gen. Philip J. Conley Jr. became commander of the AFFTC at Edwards AFB on March 8, 1978, and held the post until September 20, 1982.

The fourth and last Rockwell B-1A landed at Edwards on February 14, 1979, following its first

To take off and land repeatedly from unprepared airfields, the YC-15 AMST prototypes were outfitted with a high flotation landing gear arrangement that included a long stroke main gear to accommodate high landing sink rates. Wheel and tire sizing, spacing and pressures *were used to distribute the weight of the aircraft over a large area. The YC-15's externally blown wing flap system directed engine exhaust air under the wing and down the large, split trailing edge, double segmented flaps. McDonnell Douglas*

146

flight out of Palmdale. Further B-1A production was canceled by the Carter administration on June 30, 1977; after 347 flights and 1,895.2 total flying hours, the four B-1As were placed in limbo. Two B-1As, number two and four, were flown later as B-1B prototypes.

Of all the class acts that appeared at Edwards AFB during the 1970s, only two fighters and one jetliner entered into full-scale production:
• McDonnell Douglas F-15 Eagle
• General Dynamics F-16 Fighting Falcon
• McDonnell Douglas DC-10

Additionally, after the space shuttle *Enterprise* successfully completed five approach-and-landing tests at Edwards, the go-ahead was given to build an operational space shuttle fleet.

The 1970s were filled with a tremendous amount of activity and growth at Edwards AFB, both on and around Rogers Dry Lake. No longer considered an ungodly assignment, Edwards had metamorphosed into "the place to be" if you were a flight-test pilot or flight-test engineer. Suddenly, one could be proud to be associated with Edwards. If you worked at Edwards, you were at the edge of new and advanced aerospace technologies. More importantly, you were highly respected in the aerospace community—one of the class acts.

By mounting the engines above and ahead of the wing's leading edge, the YC-14's infrared (heat) signature was reduced, making it a more difficult target for ground-based heat-seeking missiles. To demonstrate its ease of operation, the two YC-14s flew 369 flights with eighty-one different pilots. Note its three-segment rudder. USAF via AFFTC/HO

The space shuttle Enterprise rides "piggy-back" atop a NASA 747 carrier airplane just prior to the first of five approach-and-landing test maneuvers. Moments after this photograph was taken, the 747 released Enterprise for its unpowered glide to a landing on Rogers Dry Lake. During separation, when the 747 was in a nose-down pitch attitude, it looked as though the space shuttle dropped the 747! NASA

The Enterprise glides back to terra firma after its first approach-and-landing test release from NASA's 747 car- *rier plane. Enterprise, a test air vehicle only, never flew into space nor made a powered flight of any sort. NASA*

Enterprise's first unpowered landing on Rogers Dry Lake on September 13, 1977. Enterprise's approach- and-landing tests were so successful that the projected sixth, and final, test was canceled. NASA

The M2-F1 and a number of follow-on wingless lifting bodies opened the door that allowed America's fleet of operational space shuttles to safely and accurately return to Earth from orbit. Her,e the M2-F1 and the space shuttle Enterprise share an apron at NASA's Ames/Dryden Flight Research Facility at Edwards AFB. NASA

Looking like a soaring hawk, the fourth and last Rockwell B-1A flies near Edwards with outstretched wings. At the end of its flight-test program, it was modified to serve as the number two B-1B prototype. B-1A number two became the number one B-1B prototype. Rockwell via Chris Wamsley

On August 3, 1979, the first competitive flight test of the Boeing AGM-86B Air-Launched Cruise Missile (ALCM) was launched from a B-52 out of Edwards. In competition with the General Dynamics Tomahawk ALCM, the Boeing ALCM flew a predetermined flight path from launch through the Utah Test and Training Range (UTTR) to impact in Utah. On March 25, 1980, after a series of test launches and impacts, the Boeing version of the ALCM won the Department of Defense fly-off competition. The tenth test AGM-86B ALCM is shown flying through the UTTR corridor. Boeing

A preflight check on the DAST (Drones for Aerodynamic and Structural Testing) occurred in late 1979. The unmanned, remotely piloted vehicle (RPV) was flown from a ground-based cockpit to study the ability of advanced flight control systems to control wing flutter, which can cause structural failures in aircraft. The DAST, carried under the B-52's right wing, was turbojet-powered and subsonic. NASA

Chapter 5

Fly-by-Day and Fly-by-Night, Fly-by-Wire and Fly-by-Light
The 1980s

Indeed, throughout the decades since World War II, more major milestones in flight have been achieved in the skies above Edwards than anywhere else in the world.

While the 1970s had been filled with a series of class acts on Edwards' vast stage—everything from a new wide-bodied jetliner to the space shuttle *Enterprise*—the 1980s would be the decade of an electronic revolution within the aerospace community. The development of advanced all-weather electronics allowed aircraft to fly under all weather conditions day or night, and digital fly-by-wire and fly-by-light computer-generated flight control systems allowed aircraft to fly without be-

A NASA pilot pedals the Gossamer Albatross along the shore of Rogers Dry Lake just after sunrise—the Mojave

Desert winds don't blow as hard that time of day. Bicycles function as chase vehicles. NASA

ing stable about the three axes: pitch (nose-up/nose-down), roll (wingtips-up/wingtips-down) and yaw (nose-left/nose-right). The electronic revolution also allowed attack, bomber, and fighter aircraft to deliver their ordnance precisely with sophisticated laser-guidance systems. Advanced 1980s electronics allowed aircraft to fly-by-day and fly-by-night, fly-by-wire and fly-by-light. It was the electronic revolution at Edwards in the 1980s that led to the precise night strikes in Desert Storm.

1980

In early-1980, if one did not know better, it appeared that aeronautics had taken a giant step backward at Edwards AFB. Indeed, with the arrival of the human-powered Gossamer Albatross, it seemed more like the late-1800s than the late-1900s.

The Gossamer Albatross, a lightweight, hu-man-powered airplane, was guided and pedaled by Bryan Allen in a successful crossing of the English Channel on June 12, 1979, in two hours, fifty-five minutes. Allen won the Kremer Prize for flying the first human-powered air vehicle across that famed channel. NASA subsequently leased the Gossamer Albatross for flight testing, which was completed on April 9, 1980. During the six-week program, seventeen actual data-gathering flights plus ten other flights were flown at Edwards AFB as part of the joint NASA Langley/Ames-Dryden flight research program. Results from the program were used to study the unusual aerodynamic, performance, stability, and control characteristics of large, lightweight, low-speed aircraft for possible application to future high-altitude aircraft.

The first McDonnell Douglas KC-10A Extender arrived at Edwards for ongoing flight-test and evaluation activities in July 1980. Previously, the

The premier McDonnell Douglas KC-10A Extender, winner of the earlier Advanced Tanker/Cargo Aircraft or ATCA contest, returns to Long Beach after flight test *and evaluations at Edwards AFB. The KC-10A beat Boeing's 747-based entry in a hard-fought competition.* McDonnell Douglas via Mike Machat Illustration

KC-10, a derivative of the DC-10, had won the Advanced Tanker/Cargo Aircraft (ATCA) competition over Boeing's ATCA entry, a derivative of its 747. As a result, McDonnell Douglas built sixty production KC-10s.

1981

Following the five successful approach-and-landing tests of the space shuttle *Enterprise* in the late-1970s, the first operational space shuttle—*Columbia*—was cleared for orbital flight.

On April 14, 1981, following its first orbital mission, the space shuttle *Columbia* landed safely on Rogers Dry Lake. This marked the first time in history that an orbital vehicle had left the Earth under rocket power and returned on the wings of an aircraft. It was a big media day at Edwards, with many thousands of spectators cheering the historic event.

The first operational space shuttle, Columbia, returns to earth for a safe landing on Rogers Dry Lake after its first mission into Earth orbit. NASA

After the Carter administration canceled B-1A production in 1977, money was made available for continued flight test and evaluation of the four B-1A air vehicles that had been built. Nearly 1,900 total flight-test hours would be rolled up between them, with the B-1A flight-test program ending on April 29, 1981. It was hailed as one of the most successful, mishap-free flight-test programs ever.

In early- and mid-1981, NASA's AD-1 (Ames-Dryden-1) oblique-wing aircraft—which was capable of pivoting its wing in-flight from 0 to 60deg—underwent a series of flights at Edwards. At lower flight speeds, the wing was oriented perpendicular to the fuselage, which provided efficient, quiet operation for takeoffs and landings as well as for low-speed cruise flights. The concept offered good low-speed stability and control characteristics and did not require complex high-lift devices. The engine thrust required for takeoff was substantially reduced, which resulted in quieter operation during takeoff and landing. For high-speed flights, the wing was pivoted fore and aft to form oblique angles up to 60deg with the AD-1's fuselage. In other words, its right wing was swept forward up to 60deg while its left wing was swept aftward up to 60deg, or vice versa. Studies indicated that this "scissor-wing" platform permitted improved high-speed flight performance. As the AD-1 flew faster, wing pivot to an oblique angle decreased drag, increased speed, and allowed longer range for the same expenditures of fuel. The AD-1 was powered by two small 220lb-thrust turbojets and was capable of 150 to 200mph. NASA test pilots Fitz Fulton and Thomas McMurtry flew it. Although a Super-

The NASA AD-1 flies near Edwards with its oblique wing fully pivoted. In this configuration, the right wing is swept forward and the left wing is swept aftward. NASA

The number one service-test General Dynamics YF-16 flies near Edwards AFB in its new guise as the Control Configured Vehicle or CCV testbed. Its ventral winglets, or small canard foreplanes, one on either side of the engine air inlet, afforded this Fighting Falcon unprecedented maneuverability and agility. USAF

sonic Oblique Wing Airplane was proposed, based on a modified F-8 Crusader, it never came to pass.

Following its second orbital space flight mission, the space shuttle *Columbia* touched down on Rogers Dry Lake on November 14, 1981. With this flight, the main concept of the space shuttle test program had been fully realized: The era of re-usable spacecraft had dawned.

1982

The fly-by-light USAF A-7D, featuring a single optical fiber as a data link in its computer-driven digital flight-control system, made its first flight at Edwards on March 24, 1982. By May 21, this modified A-7D had flown another twenty times with its unique fiber optics subsystem engaged. Suddenly, aircraft could fly by wire and fly by light.

On July 4, 1982, space shuttle *Columbia*, descending from its fourth orbital mission, landed on the main concrete runway for the first time at Edwards. This marked a major milestone in the shuttle program because it demonstrated that space vehicles could be safely recovered on conventional runways such as the one at the Kennedy Space Center in Florida. Today, thanks to this Edwards demonstration, space shuttle recoveries are common at Kennedy Space Center.

Following its first flight at Fort Worth, Texas, on July 10, 1982, the General Dynamics-modified Advanced Fighter Technology Integration (AFTI) F-16 was ferried to Edwards for further flight-test evaluations. This was a follow-on to the earlier AFTI F-111 program, and a follow-, follow-on to the Controlled Configured Vehicle (CCV) F-16 program, likewise performed at Edwards AFB.

After transport from Northrop's Hawthorne facility to Edwards AFB, the number one F-20 Tigershark was prepared for flight test. On August 30, 1982, with Northrop test pilot Russell J. "Russ" Scott at the controls, the first of three F-20s made a very successful first flight. As a Mach two follow-on to the Mach one F-5 series, the premier F-20

The Transonic Aircraft Technology or TACT F-111 was equipped with a special flight control system and other changes to investigate flight through the transonic speed regime by an airplane with variable-geometry wings. NASA

The Advanced Fighter Technology Integration or AFTI F-16 program was carried out to integrate and demonstrate new technologies for next-generation close air support and battlefield air-interdiction aircraft. Its canards allowed flat turns and fuselage pointing. NASA

The first of three Northrop F-20 Tigershark aircraft banks toward Rogers Dry Lake during one of its many sorties. Based on Northrop's F-5E Tiger 2, but with a higher thrust F404 jet engine and other design improvements, the F-20 was a fantastic performer with an exceptional climb rate. Northrop

The first of two B-1B prototypes, formerly B-1A prototype number two, lifts off on its first flight at Edwards AFB at the beginning of the B-1B test program. Unfortunately, this airplane later crashed, killing Rockwell test pilot Doug Benefield. Rockwell via Chris Wamsley

The first of 100 production B-1B Lancers banks sharply to the right while climbing up and away from a low-alti- *tude pass over the main runway at Edwards; wings are fully swept aftward.* Rockwell via Chris Wamsley

was designated F-5G. Scott, in a limited demonstration of the Tigershark's potential, effortlessly hit 1.04 Mach number on its first flight. Respectively, F-20 numbers two and three made their first flights at Edwards on August 26, 1983, and May 6, 1984. Although the Tigershark was everything it was supposed to be, and was even promoted by now-Brig. Gen. Chuck Yeager, the F-20 program was terminated; a fourth F-20, in early construction, was not completed.

On September 21, 1982, USAF Maj. Gen. Peter W. Odgers became commander of the AFFTC; he served until July 8, 1985.

1983–1984

After the Reagan administration had revived the B-1 program in 1980, two of four B-1As in storage at Edwards (B-1A number two and B-1A num-

ber four) were modified to serve as prototypes of the improved B-1B. Thus, the B-1B flight-test era began prior to an actual B-1B flight. The first B-1B prototype was successfully flight tested at Edwards on March 23, 1983, and the second example first flew on July 30, 1984. In less than two-and-one-half months from the latter date, the first production B-1B would fly.

Tragedy struck the B-1B program on August 29, 1984, when B-1B prototype number one (formerly B-1A prototype number two) was lost in a Mojave Desert crash near Edwards. Though its emergency four-man escape capsule jettisoned, it impacted too hard, and the force of the landing killed Doug Benefield (then chief test pilot for Rockwell International's North American Aircraft Division). The other three crewmen, though seriously injured, survived the ordeal. A malfunction

161

in the automated fuel transfer system caused a stall which led to the crash.

Work on the space shuttle program continued with a required night landing at Edwards on September 5, 1983, at 12:40 a.m. This night mission was the third flight of the space shuttle *Challenger*. (The *Challenger* was lost just after liftoff on January 28, 1986, when it exploded, killing its entire seven-person crew.)

The first of 100 production B-1B Lancer airplanes arrived at Edwards on October 18, 1984, following a successful three-hour, twenty-minute flight from Rockwell's Palmdale facility. Since 100 B-1Bs would be built, the type was originally dubbed *Centurion*. However, because of its role as a penetration bomber, it was officially named Lancer, a description of its unstoppable flight into the heart of enemy airspace.

The number one Grumman X-29A Forward-Swept Wing Advanced Technology Demonstrator airplane made its first flight on December 14, 1984 with Grumman chief test pilot Charles A. "Chuck" Sewell in the pilot's seat. This marked the first time in nearly ten years that an experimental—"X-series"—research program had flown at Edwards AFB. It also marked the first time in aviation history that an airplane had taken to the air on *thin* supercritical airfoil wings made of composite materials that swept forward. The last time an X-series air vehicle had flown at Edwards was when the X-24B made its last flight on November 26, 1975.

1985–1986

Command of Edwards switched hands on July 9, 1985, with USAF Maj. Gen. William T. Twinting taking the helm until July 22, 1988.

Still undergoing various systems test and evaluation processes at Edwards, the Rockwell B-1B Lancer is optimized for both conventional and nuclear weapons delivery. Fully operational with the USAF Air Combat Command, the B-1B, with its limited low observable, or stealth, *capabilities has now begun to replace venerable Boeing B-52G/H Stratofortress aircraft. For example, the 366th Composite Wing at Mountain Home AFB, Idaho, has just begun to receive B-1Bs as it starts to retire its fleet of B-52s. Rockwell*

After taking off from Edwards on September 13, 1985, USAF Maj. Wilbert D. "Doug" Pearson guided his F-15 Eagle into proper position and, for the first time in aviation history, fired an anti-satellite missile at an orbiting target in space. An explosion in the silence of space signaled the missile's success.

On October 15, 1985, Fairchild-Republic chief test pilot James Martinez guided the proposed "Next Generation Trainer," the Fairchild-Republic T-46A, through a successful sixty-five minute first flight, achieving an altitude of 15,000ft and a speed of 262.5mph. Good as the T-46A was, funds for it were not forthcoming. In March 1987, after three T-46As had been delivered to the USAF, the program was canceled.

Three days after the first flight of the T-46A, the first flight of the F-111 Mission Adaptive Wing (MAW) airplane was accomplished. This General Dynamics F-111A—formerly the F-111 Transonic Aircraft Technology (TACT) and the F-111 Advanced Fighter Technology Integration (AFTI) aircraft—had been modified by Boeing to incorporate a wing which allowed the curvature of the leading and trailing edges to be varied in flight. The F-111 MAW airplane was to fly with optimum wing curvatures for subsonic, transonic, and supersonic speeds to investigate the potential for greater flight efficiency. The F-111 MAW's first of fifty-eight total flights was on October 18, 1985.

In August 1986 at NASA's Ames-Dryden FRF at Edwards AFB, one of the most unusual flight vehicles ever was rolled out. The goal of the X-wing was to create an aircraft with the vertical flight characteristics of a helicopter and the horizontal cruise capability of a conventional aircraft.

NASA pilot Ed Schneider, flying NASA number 840, an F/A-18 Hornet research airplane specially instrumented and equipped for high angle of attack flight research, performs a functional check flight at Edwards, circa 1987. Flying chase in NASA number 811, an F-104 Starfighter, is NASA research pilot Charles G. "Gordon" Fullerton. NASA

When the main rotor was stopped in flight, the four large blades were to provide aerodynamic lift assistance to the stubby conventional wings extending from the X-Wing's lower fuselage. The air vehicle was developed by Sikorsky Aircraft for a joint NASA/ DARPA (Defense Advanced Research Projects Agency) program. Taxi tests and initial low-altitude flight tests without the rotor attached were carried out at Ames-Dryden FRF before the program was terminated in 1988. The reason for the end of X-Wing tests is unclear. It is assumed, however, that the advent of the Bell-Boeing V-22 Osprey program might be the reason.

Edwards again played host to aviation history on December 23, 1986. Nine days, three minutes, and forty-four seconds after taking off from Edwards, Richard Rutan and Jeana Yeager touched down on Rogers Dry Lake after completing the first nonstop, un-refueled flight around the world. The Rutan-built airplane was an experimental appropriately named *Voyager*. They flew a total distance—Edwards-to-Edwards—of 24,986.727mi at an average speed of 115.65mph.

1988

A record number of flights for an X-series air vehicle was established June 8, 1988, when NASA test pilot Rogers E. Smith flew the number one Grumman X-29A on its 200th flight. The trio of X-15s, which previously held the record, flew a total of 199 flights.

USAF Maj. Gen. John P. Schoeppner Jr. became base commander on July 23, 1988, serving until August 30, 1991.

The first of two Grumman X-29As completed the 242nd and final flight of a funded program, on December 8, 1988. A total of 178.5 flying hours had been completed, with NASA's Rogers Smith making the last flight.

continued on page 166

The X-Wing aircraft at rest on a ramp near NASA's Ames-Dryden Flight Research Facility at Edwards AFB. Oddly, though the aircraft was not tested with its large main rotor in place, it is installed here. Note its stubby wings. NASA

Colonel Harry C. Walker III

USAF Col. Harry C. Walker III was Chief, Special Projects Division, USAF Test Pilot School at Edwards AFB when he wrote the author this letter on March 16, 1990. Walker was a USAF X-29A program manager and test pilot before he moved on to become commander—fighter pilot and test pilot—of the 604th ASOC Squadron at Camp Red Cloud in South Korea. Walker, as with many other USAF command and test pilots, has flown the very latest and very best fighter aircraft in the inventory.

"When I checked in with the AFFTC X-29A Program Office at Edwards AFB, I was greeted with: 'Welcome to the X-29A program. You'll be our next (second) Air Force Flight Test Center X-29A program manager and test pilot. At this time, we don't have time to give you a dedicated sortie for training. We're just going to go for it. Get as much simulator and cockpit time as you want and let us know when you'll be ready. Your first flight will be an envelope expansion to 1.10 Mach number at 30,000ft.' So much for in-flight training time before the biggest flight of my life. I was told: 'Go ahead and feel the airplane out as you climb to 30,000ft, but

fuel is critical so don't take too much time. We need to hit the data points so we can get on with envelope expansion.' I knew at that point that this program would be unlike any program I'd been on before.

"The X-29A program was a great step forward for the experimental aircraft community. We hadn't flown a new X aircraft in some ten years and the push to get the X-29A into the air more often was a benefit to the entire aerospace community. Experimental aircraft programs need to be an ongoing effort to allow experimenters the opportunity to investigate what the paper concepts will do in real life. The role of experimental aircraft in the evolution of flight is often misunderstood or undervalued. For relatively low cost, we can develop and validate, in-flight, key technologies for future use. X aircraft are win-win situations—if you find that the technology isn't ready for production or viable at all, you still come out ahead because (to paraphrase Mr. Edison), 'failed experiments tell us what not to do.'

"The X-29A program is a unique and wonderful program. It allows us to look into numerous aircraft technologies and flight-test methodologies that can and will be used in the future. The techniques developed and

Walker poses by X-29A number one. *USAF*

refined during the flight testing of the X-29A give the aerospace community new and refined tools for data acquisition and evaluation. The technologies on the aircraft can be used to reduce total drag as well as enhance future fighter maneuverability.

"People wonder why the forward-swept wing works and why we should build this type of aircraft. The answer is: 'Why not?' In the past, we were restricted to aftward-swept wings due to material constraints. With improved materials—in this case, advanced composite materials—we were able to build a wing that can be "tuned" to do the job and still provide adequate strength-to-weight margin. The benefit is reduced drag in the transonic speed regime [600–800mph]. Drag reduction is a hard thing to nail down due to the numerous contributors to total drag, but in the case of the X-29A, the net reduction in drag due to lift when compared to an aftward-swept wing is considerable—20–40 percent. This degree of performance increase can easily be translated into improved fighter performance and maneuverability. As history tells, forward-swept wings go back to the earliest subsonic, transonic, and supersonic designs. It is only recently that we have the technology to build and fly them in the supersonic speed regime. We had been strapped to the subsonic speed regime prior to the advent of the X-29A.

"The other major technologies in the X-29A were included in the test program to complement the forward-swept wing. These made the X-29A possible and, at the same time, allowed the program to explore a multifaceted problem. The variable camber, three-surface lift, and full authority close-coupled canard foreplanes are all technologies that can—and I think *should*—be incorporated into future fighter design.

"I've often been asked how it feels to fly an airplane that relies on a computer to 'stay in the air.' It feels just like any other modern fighter. The state of aerodynamic stability and control allows us to now employ a central processor to enhance the control of the air vehicle. In other words, the computer in the X-29A is there to help the pilot get more out of the aircraft. Similar advances have occurred in the past. We went from wing warping to ailerons, added hydraulic boosting of flying control surfaces, and then went to a hydromechanical control surface. At each step along the way, these advances gave the pilot more precise and absolute control over the air vehicle. The addition of a computer is nothing more than an evolutionary step in the process of gaining control over the aircraft. Digital flight control systems are here to stay and will enable us to extract more performance and control from our aircraft.

"My few flights in the number one X-29A were a wonderful experience. I was privileged to work with all the members of the test team from the U.S. Air Force, NASA, and Grumman. It is rare in this day to have the opportunity to do envelope expansion and performance testing on a new airplane. Grumman's X-29A performs well and has very few maintenance problems. Our major problems stemmed from instrumentation and the desire to gather large amounts of data on each sortie—the aircraft is indeed a flying laboratory. Overall, X-29A performance can be equated to an F-16, but with the caveat that it is a one-of-a-kind experimental aircraft and not a missioned production fighter [like General Dynamic's F-16 Fighting Falcon]. There are no weapons systems or avionics. The handling qualities improved over the span of my thirty-three flights to the point that they were adequate for the research role but were not optimized for a front-line fighter."

continued from page 164

On December 22, 1988, the F-111 MAW airplane completed its fifty-ninth and last flight. During a total of 144.9 flying hours, its best speed was 1.4 Mach number and its best altitude was 42,100ft. Reductions in air drag from 8 to 20 percent were noted during the tests, as was a 20 percent reduction in wing bending during maneuvers. All in all, four NASA and six USAF pilots flew the F-111 MAW before the program's end.

1989

Specially fitted with two-dimensional, thrust-vectoring engine exhaust nozzles and canard foreplanes, the McDonnell Douglas F-15 SMTD (STOL and Maneuver Technology Demonstrator) took off on May 10, 1989, to begin a 100-flight, thirteen-month test program at Edwards. The exhaust nozzles, also fitted with thrust reversers, allowed the F-15 SMTD to demonstrate improved short takeoff and landing (STOL) and in-flight maneuverability.

With NASA's Stephen D. "Steve" Ishmael at the controls, the number two Grumman X-29A Forward-Swept Wing Advanced Technology Demonstrator made its first flight at Edwards AFB on May 23.

Like the boomerang it resembled, a Northrop flying wing bomber returned to Edwards AFB on July 17, 1989, albeit some forty years after the USAF tossed it. The Northrop B-2 Advanced Technology Bomber (ATB), was flown from Northrop's Palmdale plant by Northrop's Bruce J. Hinds and copiloted by USAF's Col. Richard S. Couch.

On September 10, the Air Force Anechoic Facility or AFAF at Edwards AFB entered operation. The mission of the AFAF is to provide the USAF with the capability to test the integrated avionic systems of large aircraft such as bombers within a shielded and secure environment. It was first used to support the development of the B-1B defensive avionics system. At 70,200sq-ft, it's the free world's largest anechoic chamber, featuring a shielded chamber area measuring some 264ft by 250ft with

NASA investigated laminar flow technology to help improve the flow of air over an aircraft's wing at sustained supersonic speeds. To do this, it flew both F-16XL air- *craft, on loan from the USAF, throughout fiscal year 1990. NASA*

a 70ft-high ceiling (the outer dimensions). It's literally a building within a building.

The 1980s at Edwards culminated with the first captive carry test of *Pegasus* under the right wing of a NASA B-52, on November 9, 1989. *Pegasus* is a space launch booster capable of launching small payloads into Earth orbit.

The fly-by-day and fly-by-night, fly-by-wire and fly-by-light 1980s was a ten-year period dedicated fully to the advancement of the state-of-the-art in both aeronautics and astronautics. It was an era in which the entire aerospace community excelled. And from their respective tests in the 1980s

at Edwards AFB, a number of new aircraft went into full-scale production. These included:
• McDonnell Douglas KC-10 Extender
• America's space shuttle fleet
• Rockwell B-1B Lancer
• Northrop B-2

The electronic revolution in the 1980s had concluded. However, with carry-over programs such as the ongoing B-2 development and others, the upcoming 1990s promised to generate ten more years of aero/astro progress at Edwards AFB. Indeed, the AFFTC was heading "Toward the Unexplored."

The Mission Adaptive Wing or MAW F-111 demonstrated automatic leading- and trailing-edge wing bents without the leading-edge slat and trailing-edge flat splits normally found between slat, flap, and wing surfaces. NASA

Left
The number one X-29A poses on Rogers Dry Lake. It was flown to investigate its forward-swept wing, close-coupled canard configuration, and other advanced technologies. The number two X-29A investigated the type's high angle of attack characteristics and other aerodynamic functions. NASA

Had it been ordered into production, the Fairchild-Republic T-46A (called the Next Generation Trainer or NGT) would have been the USAF's replacement for the venerable Cessna T-37. Piloted by Fairchild-Republic chief test pilot James Martinez on October 15, 1985, the first T-46A is shown during its maiden flight at Edwards. USAF via AFFTC/HO

Left
Retired USAF Brig. Gen. Chuck Yeager gained fame as the first man to fly an airplane faster than the speed of sound. Yeager received his pilot wings and appointment as a flight officer on March 10, 1943, and retired from USAF active duty on March 1, 1975. In addition to his historic penetration of the sound barrier on October 14, 1947, Yeager also earned double ace status with thirteen kills during WW-II. He was also commandant of the USAF Test Pilot School (then Aerospace Research Pilot School) at Edwards, beginning in 1962. Whether wing commander or vice-commander of the 7th Air Force, Yeager did nothing but excel during his USAF career. USAF

The F-15 SMTD flies near the housing area at Edwards AFB. Amazingly, with its thrust vectoring/reversing two-dimensional exhaust nozzles and canard foreplanes, *this fighter-type can take off in 1,000ft or less and land and stop in less than 1,250ft. Canard foreplanes are modified F/A-18 Hornet tailplanes.* **McDonnell Douglas**

Shown is USAF Maj. Doug Pearson flying his F-15A Eagle around Edwards, circa 1985. On September 13, 1985, Pearson successfully guided this F-15 into position and, for the first time in history, fired the anti-satellite *missile (mounted underneath the airplane) at an orbiting satellite in space. The target was hit and destroyed.* USAF

If only Jack Northrop could see this version of his original concept of a flying-wing bomber. The B-2 of today is *the epitome of his shape of wings to come, the essence of all he believed.* Northrop

Between August 1986 and January 1988, NASA conducted taxi tests and initial low-altitude flight tests without the main rotor attached as shown. NASA

The Pegasus space launch booster was rolled-out by its manufacturer Orbital Sciences Corporation for its first public viewing on August 10, 1989. The roll-out occurred at OSC's assembly building at NASA's Ames-Dryden Flight Research Facility at Edwards. Pegasus, capable of launching small payloads into low earth orbit, is air-launched from beneath a NASA B-52 mother plane's right wing. The roll-out Pegasus shown was a test article, rather than an actual launch vehicle. NASA

The number one B-1B in the AFFTC's Anechoic Chamber at Edwards AFB. Rockwell via Chris Wamsley

NASA B-52 008 lifts off on the first captive flight of a Pegasus air-launched space booster, a device already used to successfully place small satellites into earth orbit. NASA

Chapter 6

Toward the Unexplored

The 1990s and Beyond

It isn't the physical danger; I know I can get the plane back. It's just that it's a challenging mission, and it's before your colleagues, and you have one chance to be a hero . . . and a thousand chances to be a bum.

—Bill Dana

The 1990s began with the anticipated arrivals of an advanced jetliner (the McDonnell Douglas MD-11 and C-17A Globemaster III), an advanced attack airplane (the LTV (Ling/Temco/Vought) YA-7F), and a pair of service-test advanced tactical fighter aircraft (the Lockheed/Boeing YF-22A and the Northrop/McDonnell Douglas YF-23A). Before the end of 1990, all four types had successfully flown through the skies above Edwards. Additionally, the number two B-2 arrived. While an electronic revolution had taken place at Edwards in the 1980s, the 1990s and beyond will be the period when all these advanced avionics fully mature. For example, the proposed X-30A National Aerospace Plane (NASP) is scheduled to take wing from Edwards sometime before the year 2000. Powered by

The first McDonnell Douglas MD-11 tri-jet jetliner's landing gear begins to retract as it takes off on another test hop at Edwards AFB. The type easily passed Federal Aviation Administration certification and is now being delivered to airline customers. McDonnell Douglas

The Vought, formerly LTV (Ling-Temco-Vought), YA-7F Corsair III was a service-test close Air Support/Battlefield Air Interdiction (CAS/BIA) airplane capable of one-plus Mach number speed in level flight. The supersonic YA-7F was created from a pair of modified subsonic A-7D Corsair 2 aircraft, which in turn had been created from the redesigned supersonic F-8 Crusader. The YA-7F, though not proceeded with, demonstrated a unique configuration, whereby one basic airframe—the F-8—created the A-7 series (subsonic), and the supersonic YA-7F. Talk about coming full circle! USAF via AFFTC/HO

scramjet engines, the proposed X-30A, based on a lifting body configuration, is to attain low-Earth orbit before its reentry and landing. Manned by a crew of two, the proposed NASP will usher in Edwards' next decades.

1990

On January 10, 1990, after lifting off at Long Beach, the first McDonnell Douglas MD-11 three-jet jetliner made a successful test hop prior to its planned landing at Edwards. Flown by John I. Miller, the MD-11, a competitor of Boeing's upcoming 777 four-jet jetliner, reached an altitude of 25,000ft and a speed of 450mph.

Two days later, after being ferried to Edwards AFB from Ling-Temco-Vought's Dallas, Texas, facility, the first of two service-test LTV YA-7F derivative A-7D Corsair 2 aircraft began a flight-test and evaluation program with its first takeoff/landing sortie at Edwards. It was flown by USAF Lt. Col. Mark Prill. LTV's Jim Read had made its first flight at Dallas on November 29, 1989. YA-7F number two arrived at Edwards on April 6, 1990. Both went on to enjoy an extremely good flight-test program before the type was canceled due to budget cuts.

The first of two Northrop/McDonnell Douglas YF-23As, sporting a pair of Pratt & Whitney YF119 engines, rolled out at Edwards AFB on June 22, 1990. This was a first of sorts, as no new aircraft had been unveiled to the public at Edwards since the Lockheed YF-12A in 1964. After a series of low- and medium-speed taxi trials begun on July 7, the first of two YF-23As successfully completed its first flight on August 27, with Northrop Advanced Tactical Fighter (ATF) chief test pilot Paul Metz at the controls.

Powered by two General Electric YF120 engines, the first of two Lockheed/Boeing YF-22As was rolled-out *inside* Lockheed Advanced Development Company's Palmdale facility at USAF Plant 42 on August 29, 1990. And after a series of low- and medium-speed taxi trials at Palmdale ended on September 27, it made its first flight on September 29, landing at Edwards AFB. Lockheed ATF chief test pilot David L. "Dave" Ferguson was under glass.

Under separate contracts, each ATF team provided two ATF service-test aircraft, and each team powered each one of their respective aircraft with a different propulsion system, either two Pratt &

Powered by two Pratt & Whitney YF119 engines, the number one service-test Northrop/McDonnell Douglas YF-23A Grey Ghost poses in mid-air to flaunt its stealthy configuration. Its tailplanes, which double as vertical and horizontal stabilizers, are unique. **Northrop**

Whitney YF119s or two General Electric YF120s. It would be a winner-take-all competition where the best ATF airframe and powerplant combination would prevail.

YF-23A number two, powered by two YF120s, and YF-22A number two, powered by two YF119s, made their first flights on October 26 and 30, 1990, respectively. The former flew at Edwards AFB and the latter at Palmdale; both YF-22As landed at Edwards after their first flights. The number two YF-23A was piloted by Northrop test pilot Jim Sandberg, and the number two YF-22A was flown by Lockheed test pilot Tom Morgenfeld.

To complete their scheduled flight-test activi-ties, both YF-22As flew a total of seventy-four flights during a ninety-one-day period; both YF-23As flew a total of fifty flights in 104 days.

During their flights, both ATF types demon-strated top speeds in excess of 2.5 Mach number, supercruise (supersonic cruise without afterburn-ing) speeds above 1.5 Mach number, unprecedent-ed maneuverability and agility, excellent stability and control, and impressive turnaround times be-tween flights—often two or more on the same day! Still, as good as both designs were, only one could win, and on April 23, 1991, the Pratt & Whitney YF119-powered YF-22A advanced. It soon re-sumed additional flight-test activities at Edwards.

Powered by two General Electric YF120 engines, the number one service-test Lockheed/Boeing YF-22A Light-ning II advanced tactical fighter shows off its sporty lines. Production F-22s will have shorter noses and smaller vertical tails. Lockheed

Powered by two General Electric YF120 engines, the number two service-test YF-23A illustrates its right side, in-flight profile. All movable tailplanes act as stabilators (combined horizontal stabilizers and elevators), vertical stabilizers, and rudders. The forward fuselage appears to be attached to the wings rather than the wings being attached to it. AFFTC/PA

Powered by two Pratt & Whitney YF119s, the number two service-test YF-22A (the winning ATF combination) flies near Edwards on one of its numerous test hops.

This airplane was selected by USAF as replacement to the F-15 Eagle beginning in 2002. Lockheed

The number one (background) and number two YF-23As fly in formation showing their unique configurations. Sometimes it seems a shame that there has to be a loser, *for the F-23, in appearance and other aspects, was a winner.* Northrop

In September 1990, the number two Northrop B-2 ATB arrived at Edwards following its first flight from Palmdale; B-2 number three arrived in June 1991.

1991–1992

The number one B-2 completed its first cross-country deployment on June 5, 1991, as it flew from Edwards to Andrews AFB in Maryland in support of Operation Cherry Blossom. While at Andrews, the B-2 Stealth bomber was placed on display with a Lockheed F-117 Stealth fighter, a Convair/McDonnell Douglas AGM-129A Advanced Cruise Missile, and a Lockheed YF-22A as part of what the media called "Stealth Week."

USAF Brig. Gen. Roy D. Bridges Jr. became base commander on August 31, 1991. On June 18, 1993, after some two years, Bridges relinquished command to Brig. Gen. Richard L. Engel. Engel

was still center commander at this writing.

Following a successful two-hour twenty-three-minute flight from Long Beach, the first McDonnell Douglas C-17 landed on September 15, 1991, for continued testing. It was piloted by McDonnell Douglas test pilot William "Bill" Casey and copiloted by USAF Lt. Col. George London.

On September 30, 1991, the number two Grumman X-29A flew the last flight of the type's original flight-test schedules. The two X-29As' flight program, having flown 302 total flights without serious or even moderate mishap, has to go down as one of the most successful of any X-type. The last flight of an X-29A (number two) occurred on August 28, 1992, following an additional USAF-funded program of sixty flights; prior to this program, the two aircraft had flown 242 times.

During a short side-by-side flight from Palmdale in December 1991, the two Rockwell/Messer-schmitt-Bolkow-Blohm (MBB) X-31A Enhanced Fighter Maneuverability (EFM) research aircraft landed at Edwards for a joint Rockwell/MBB, USN and NASA flight-test program.

On April 25, 1992, the very same service-test YF-22A that had earlier won the ATF competition, crash-landed at Edwards AFB. The airplane was on a scheduled flight test in support of the F-22 Engineering and Manufacturing Development (EMD) program, formerly known as Full Scale Development (FSD). Lockheed test pilot Tom Morgenfeld, had accomplished one low approach and had nearly completed a second. As he began to go around following the second low approach, the airplane experienced severe pitch (nose-up/nose-down) oscillations, impacted the runway landing gear up, skidded several thousand feet, and caught fire. Morgenfeld egressed the plane on the ground with only minor injuries, and the plane, though damaged, was not destroyed.

The fourth McDonnell Douglas C-17 arrived at Edwards on September 7, 1992, after a one-hour, thirty-minute flight from Long Beach. Respectively, C-17s number two and three arrived on May 19 and June 21, 1992. As of September 7, 1992, the four C-17s at Edwards had a combined total of 474.5 flight-test hours in 139 flights.

There was a momentous occasion at Edwards AFB on October 2, 1992. With ninety-two-year-old Lt. Gen. Laurence C. "Bill" Craigie (USAF, retired) in attendance, in addition to a large number of Jet Pioneer's Association members and Brig. Gen. Charles E. "Chuck" Yeager (USAF, retired) in attendance, the fiftieth anniversary of jet flight was

Among the numerous NASA aircraft based at Edwards are these two naval fighters: a McDonnell Douglas F/A-18 Hornet, foreground; and, a Grumman F-14 Tomcat (NASA numbers 841 and 834 respectively). Recently, NASA obtained both Northrop YF-23A aircraft that par- *ticipated with two Lockheed YF-22As in the Advanced Tactical Fighter (ATF) fly-off at Edwards. The latter aircraft won the hard-fought and very close fly-off competition in early 1991. NASA*

celebrated. In conjunction with the Jet Pioneer's Association and the Air Force Flight Test Center, there was a ceremony on the lake bed at North Base (probably the first time that the general public was ever allowed there) and an aerial demonstration of the F-15, F-16, and the F-117. Furthermore, General Yeager flew a two-seat F-16 in a supersonic simulation of his October 14, 1947, accomplishment in the Bell X-1. The event celebrated General Craigie's first flight of the Bell XP-59A Airacomet, America's first jet-powered airplane. It celebrated General Electric's model I-A, America's first turbojet engine. And, last but not least, it celebrated all the men and women in the Jet Pioneer's Association of the United States of America. (On a sad note, Lt. Gen. "Bill" Craigie died on February 27, 1994, at the age of ninety-four. Craigie entered the U.S. Army Air Service in the 1920s and had literally "seen it all" in aviation advancements for more than seven decades.)

Three days later, October 5, 1992, the fifth B-2 landed at Edwards after its first flight of just under four hours from Palmdale. As of that date, the five B-2s at Edwards have flown 815 total hours in 176 flights. The number six B-2 arrived in 1993.

After an uneventful flight from Edwards AFB to Whiteman AFB in Missouri, the first operational B-2 (number eight)—named *Spirit of Missouri*—was delivered to the Air Combat Command's 509th Bomb Wing. It was piloted by the 509th's Lt. Col. John Belanger. The copilot and mission commander was ACC commander Gen. Mike Loh. In May 1994, on another flight from Edwards, the number ten B-2 was delivered to the 509th BW.

The number one (background) and number two YF-22As fly in formation. The way the F-22's stabilators fit into the trailing edges of the wings is unique; in essence, they are close-coupled stabilators. Lockheed

Edwards' air traffic control tower as it appears today.
Author

In the 1990s, Edwards AFB will host new jet-liners like McDonnell Douglas' MD-90 twin-jet, new fighters like Lockheed's single-seat F-22A and twin-seat F-22B, new multi-service (USAF/USN/USMC) fighters like those being proposed by Boeing and others, and if all goes as planned, the X-30 and the National Aero-Space Plane.

Moreover, like the new Air Force Flight Test Center headquarters building now under construction, there will be more growth and more jobs.

Just a water stop for trains at one time, Edwards has become an indispensable place for aeronautical training.

The Future

Since its inception more than sixty years ago, the Air Force Flight Test Center at Edwards Air Force Base has played host to many amazing aviation-related advances. From speeds below Mach one to speeds far more than Mach six, from altitudes far lower than 30,000ft to altitudes surpassing 300,000ft, from straight-up flight to straight-down flight, and all kinds of flight in between, if it happened, it most likely happened at "Eddie's."

One still has to wonder, however, what will be going on at Edwards as the 20th century metamor-

The original airplane hangar at North Base as it appears today, some fifty-two years after it was built. Author

phoses into the 21st. Of late, the dark clouds of defense cuts and air base closures continue to gather over the U.S. armed forces. Yet, there remains one ray of brightness: the knowledge that ongoing activities at Edwards is crucial to our national security. With little doubt then, Edwards will be open and operating in the next century. Simply, for the continued advancement of the aeronautical and astronautical sciences—especially in the field of flight test and evaluation of new and better air and space vehicles, military or civilian—there is no better place to live and work than Edwards.

Thus, its Latin motto *Ad Inexplorata*, or Toward the Unexplored, is most appropriate for the place where visions are realized.

The McDonnell Douglas C-17, the USAF's newest airlifter, is optimized to carry large combat equipment, troops, and cargo across international distances and deliver them directly to austere airfields anywhere in the world. The first C-17 is shown taking off for the first time at Long Beach prior to its first landing at Edwards AFB. McDonnell Douglas

The Northrop B-2A, optimized for stealthy warfare, is the essence of a flying-wing aircraft—the epitome of what John K. "Jack" Nothrop envisioned as the definitive bombardment platform. Now becoming operational, the USAF Air Combat Command (509th Bomb Wing) recently received the first operational B-2 on December 17, 1993. Incidentally, that date marked the ninetieth anniversary of the Wright Brothers' first powered airplane flight. USAF

To help reduce space shuttle roll-out distances and the wear and tear of wheel braking during landings, all of the space shuttles are now equipped with braking parachutes. Here a test braking 'chute successfully unfurls behind a NASA B-52 at Edwards on July 20, 1990. Eight such tests validated the system, ulitimately reducing a space shuttle's landing roll-out distance. NASA

Prior to their respective ferry flights to the USN's flight-test facility on the East Coast, both Rockwell/MBB X-31 EFM aircraft continue (at this writing) to undergo an extensive flight-test program at Edwards. The X-31 is capable of close-in aerial combat maneuvering at very high angles of attack, and it can also perform the tricky post-stall maneuver. When their tests are completed at Edwards, they are to be moved to the Naval Air Test Center (NATC), Patuxent River, Maryland. NASA

The number two Grumman X-29 shows off its unprecedented configuration during a test hop near Edwards. Except for the spin-recovery parachute system (just aft of the vertical fin) and instrumentation, it is identical to the number one X-29A. NASA

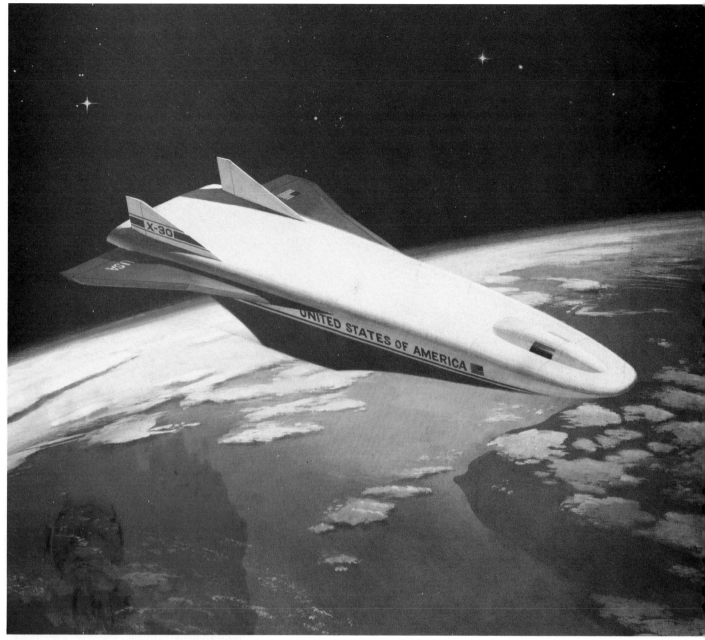

As a prelude to the National Aero-Space Plane (NASP), with flights now scheduled to start in the late 1990s, the sub-scale X-30 will launch America on a course that will maintain its aerospace lead in the world market of the 21st century. Intended to demonstrate airbreathing single-stage-to-orbit flight, the X-30 will carry two crew members, burn hydrogen fuel, take off and land conventionally from runways, have a turnaround time measured in days, and be capable of 25 Mach number (17,500mph) speed. Rockwell via Chris Wamsley

Edwards AFB
Facility Commanders

Commander	Tenure	Commander	Tenure
Glenn L. Arbogast	7/24/42 to 12/12/42	Howard M. Lane	10/19/72 to 2/24/74
Frank D. Gore	12/13/42 to 3/13/44	Robert A. Rushworth	2/25/74 to 11/3/75
Robert O. Cork	3/14/44 to 3/31/44	Thomas P. Stafford	11/4/75 to 3/7/78
Ralph A. Snavely	4/1/44 to 5/1/44	Philip J. Conley Jr.	3/8/78 to 9/20/82
Gerald E. Hoyle	5/2/44 to 12/21/44	Peter W. Odgers	9/21/82 to 7/8/85
Warren E. Maxwell	12/22/44 to 5/1/46	William T. Twinting	7/9/85 to 7/22/88
Signa A. Gilkey	5/2/46 to 8/31/49	John P. Schoeppner Jr.	7/23/88 to 8/30/91
Albert Boyd	9/7/49 to 1/28/52	Roy D. Bridges Jr.	8/31/91 to 6/18/93
J. Stanley Holtoner	2/18/52 to 5/19/57	Richard L. Engel	6/19/93 to Present
Marcus F. Cooper	7/8/57 to 2/6/59		
John W. Carpenter III	3/3/59 to 6/12/61		
Irving L. Branch[1]	6/29/61 to 1/16/66		
Ray Vandiver[2]	1/4/66 to 1/16/66		
Hugh B. Manson	1/17/66 to 12/6/68		
Alton D. Slay	12/7/68 to 7/31/70		
Robert M. White	8/1/70 to 10/18/72		

[1] Commander Branch was fatally injured January 3, 1966, when the airplane he was landing at Boeing Field crashed into Puget Sound near Seattle, Washington.

[2] Ray Vandiver stood in for Branch while Branch was TDY (temporary duty) at Boeing. Vandiver was replaced by Manson.

USAF Aircraft Test Phases

Phase I—Air Worthiness: flight test conducted by the contractor to demonstrate the aircraft's ability to fly safely.

Phase II—Contractor Compliance: flight tests, in which the Air Force test pilots fly the aircraft to determine if it meets the performance guarantees.

Phase III—Design Refinement: conducted by the contractor, using the same aircraft as in Phases I and II, to overcome deficiencies noted during the previous tests.

Phase IV—Performance and Stability: flight test to obtain detailed data on the aircraft's performance and handling qualities.

Phase V—All Weather: tests to ascertain the aircraft's limitations under adverse weather conditions.

Phase VI—Functional Development: focuses on the tactically-equipped production aircraft and identifies previously undiscovered shortcomings. Also assessed in this phase is the aircraft's durability, maintainability, logistical support, and so on.

Phase VII—Operational Suitability: also known as Employment and Suitability Testing, this phase addresses the problem areas the user experiences with the acquisition of a new system (the user being the operational command such as the Air Combat Command [ACC]). The aircraft no longer being in flight test; sometimes conducted at Edwards AFB.

Phase VIII—Unit Operational Employment Testing: similar to Phase VII, evaluates an aircraft at its first operational unit, using information gathered under actual field operating conditions with typical personnel and maintenance facilities. Not conducted at Edwards AFB.

Bibliography

Books

Angelucci, Enzo, with Bowers, Peter M. *The American Fighter*. New York, NY: Orion Books, 1987.

Bowers, Peter M. *Boeing Aircraft since 1916*. Annapolis, MD: Naval Institute Press, 1989.

Bowers, Peter M. *Curtiss Aircraft 1907–1947*. Annapolis, MD: Naval Institute Press, 1979.

Francillon, Rene J. *Grumman Aircraft since 1929*. Annapolis, MD: Naval Institute Press, 1989.

Francillon, Rene J. *Lockheed Aircraft since 1913*. Annapolis, MD: Naval Institute Press, 1987.

Francillon, Rene J. *McDonnell Douglas Aircraft since 1920: Volume I*. Annapolis, MD: Naval Institute Press, 1988.

Francillon, Rene J. *McDonnell Douglas Aircraft since 1920: Volume II*. Annapolis, MD: Naval Institute Press, 1990.

Goldberg, Alfred, ed. *A History of the United States Air Force 1907–1957*. Princetown, NJ: Van Nostrand Co., Inc., 1957.

Johnston, A.M. "Tex" with Barton, Charles. *Tex Johnston Jet Age Pilot*. New York, NY: Bantam Books, July 1992.

Knaack, Marcelle Size. *Post-World War II Fighters 1945–1973*. Washington, DC: U.S. Government Printing Office, 1985.

LeVier, Tony with Guenther, John. *Pilot*. New York, NY: Bantam Books, 1990.

Miller, Jay. *The X-Planes X-1 to X-31*. New York, NY: Orion Books, 1988.

Pace, Steve. *X-Fighters: USAF Prototype and Service Test Jet Fighters XP-59 to YF-23*. Osceola, WI: Motorbooks International Publishers and Wholesalers, 1991.

Pace, Steve. *Lockheed F-104 Starfighter*. Osceola, WI: Motorbooks International Publishers and Wholesalers, 1992.

Pace, Steve. *The Grumman X-29*. Blue Ridge Summit, PA: Tab/McGraw-Hill Books, 1991.

Pelletier, A. J. *Bell Aircraft since 1935*. Annapolis, MD: Naval Institute Press, 1992.

Stoff, Joshua. *The Thunder Factory*. Osceola, WI: Motorbooks International Publishers and Wholesalers, 1990.

Wagner, Ray. *American Combat Planes*. Garden City, NY: Doubleday and Company, Inc., 1982.

Wegg, John. *General Dynamics Aircraft and their Predecessors*. Annapolis, MD: Naval Institute Press, 1990.

Periodical Articles

Young, James O. "The Golden Age at Muroc-Edwards." *Journal of the West*, January 1991.

Military Histories

History of the Air Force Flight Test Center: Bi-annual AFFTC History Office volumes, various sections, 1954–1972.

Young, James O. *Supersonic Symposium: The Men of Mach 1*. Air Force Systems Command, 1990.

Index